QUICKB

A Comprehensive Guide to Bookkeeping
and Learning Techniques on QuickBooks
Software for Beginners

By John Kent

By reading this document, the reader agrees that under no circumstances is the author responsible for any losses, direct or indirect, which are incurred as a result of the use of information contained within this document, including, but not limited to, —errors, omissions, or inaccuracies.

Table of Contents

Introduction..**x**

Chapter One - Why Use Quickbooks?...................**1**

Self-Employed.. 1

Ease Of Use 3

Tax Prediction.. 4

Impeccable Design 5

Online Invoices And Payments.......................... 6

Managing Transactions In Quickbooks 7

Tracking Mileage... 8

Quickbooks And Taxation................................. 9

Reporting 9

Handling Invoices Inside Quickbooks..................... 10

Chapter Two - Operating Quickbooks................**13**

What Tasks Do Small Businesses Use Quickbooks For?... 14

Manage Sales And Income................................ 14

Check Expenses And Bills 14

Reporting Insights 15

Profit And Loss Report 16

Balance Sheet Report 16

Statement Of Cash Flow 16

Run Payroll 17

Track Inventory 18

Simplification Of Taxes 19

Accept Online Payments 19

Scan Receipts 20

Quickbooks Features & Pricing 21

Quickbooks Online 21

Quickbooks Desktop 22

Quickbooks Self-Employed 22

Quickbooks Mac 23

Chapter Three - Payroll 24

Payroll Setup: Data That You Need 24

Add Employee Info 26

How To Run Payroll In Quickbooks Online 32

Chapter Four - Tracking Receipts 36

What Is A Sales Receipt? 37

What Information Should Be Present On A Sales Receipt? 37

The Importance Of Receipts 40

What's The Difference Between An Invoice And A Sales Receipt? 41

Different Receipt Types For Different Industries.. 43

How To Make A Sales Receipt................................... 45

Creating Sales Receipts In Quickbooks Online 48

Managing Sales Receipts For Your Small Business 51

Chapter Five - Inventory **53**

Check Your Subscription First................................... 54

How To Set Up Inventory Parts And Non-Inventory Parts In Quickbooks 54

Set Up And Track Your Inventory 57

Ivd Or Inventory Valuation Detail Report.............. 62

Negative Item Listing Report 63

Chapter Six - Financial Statements **70**

Balance Sheet... 70

Types Of Balance Sheets 71

Generating A Balance Sheet 72

Income Statement.. 73

Revenue And Expenses... 78

Formatting Your Income Statement 84

How To Read A Cash Flow Statement.................... 93

Chapter Seven - Bookkeeping With Quickbooks 96

Quickbooks Proadvisor... 96

An Expert In Quickbooks Setup 98

Stay Up- To- Date On Tax Laws 99

Provide Financial Advice And Insights................. 100

Training For Accounting Staff 101

Focus On Growth 101

Summary 103

Choosing The Right Plan 103

Quickbooks Desktop Vs. Quickbooks Online 110

How To Choose?.. 116

Quickbooks Desktop To Quickbooks Online...... 118

Quickbooks Desktop Versions And Others 120

Quickbooks Versions... 123

How To Decide Which Quickbooks To Buy 128

Becoming A Certified Quickbooks Proadvisor 131

Taking The Certification Exam 138

Chapter Eight - Quickbooks Tips........................141

Use Proadvisor 142

Reconciling On Quickbooks 145

Backing Up Quickbooks 145

Print Checks Directly From Quickbooks 146

Paying Bills Via Quickbooks 146

Customize Your Quickbooks' Layout 147

Customize Your Icon Bar 147

Utilize Memorized Transactions 147

Use Online Banking 148

Setting Up 1099 Vendors 148

Turning Off Spellcheck 148

Restricting User Access 149

Online Payments Via Quickbooks 149

Find The History Of A Transaction 150

Linking Your Email To Quickbooks 150

Viewing Double Entries 150

Merging Similar Accounts 151

Chat With Staff 151

Offset Invoices Against Credit Notes 152

Printing Batch Invoices 152

Conclusion **153**

INTRODUCTION

The world is changing rapidly, and a lot of people have now become entrepreneurs. Many people have started their own businesses or are planning to do so. Start-up culture has now reached the grassroots. Due to this, a lot of new business people and entrepreneurs have start-ups. People keep on coming up with new ideas and plans to earn money.

Although a lot of people start new businesses every day, not all of them succeed. There are a multitude of reasons behind this including lack of planning, lack of market research, lack of business sense, lack of understanding, etc. are some of the most prominent reasons why businesses tend to fail. Another very common reason why businesses tend to fail is that new and many times experienced business owners do not know how to handle their accounts or do not consider them important enough. This is a grave error that has cost a lot of people their successful enterprises. It is thus recommended to learn as much as possible about accounting and bookkeeping.

Nowadays, thanks to the evolution of technology, there are many online and computerized bookkeeping and accounting software packages available on the market. All of these have different and interesting features that have made them quite popular. But most of these software packages are either too costly or do not have a lot of essential tools. But one software is sure to stand out from the crowd - QuickBooks.

QuickBooks is a highly advanced accounting and bookkeeping software created by Intuit. It is an interesting combination of many different accounting related functions and features in one single shell that is extremely easy to use and user-friendly as well. It helps people to stop relying excessively on spreadsheets, multiple tables, and tracking sheets as well. It performs a lot of intricate tasks automatically. It maintains a lot of accounting as well as financial tasks on a daily basis for you, automatically. Many people find filing taxes a complex and complicated process. QuickBooks can help you simplify this process because it will quickly and easily reconcile accounting figures.

One of the best things about this software is that it is highly customizable, and users can change and customize it according to their needs and requirements. Many users use a highly customized version of the program that is suited to their firm or industry.

If you are a beginner to the world of QuickBooks and find it kind of confusing, complex, or even scary, then don't worry. This book will help you learn the basics and advanced information about QuickBooks that can help you become the master of QuickBooks. It will help you learn the basics that can be used to maintain your finances and record your business dealings as well. It should be noted that QuickBooks is not just a program that records your daily transactions and deals. It can also be used for various other purposes as well. For instance, it can help you keep track of your finances, keep track of your customers, and keep track of your receipts and payments as well. This program contains everything that a new and budding (or even an expert) businessman may need. This book will get you started in the world of QuickBooks. It will help you study QuickBooks in depth.

Let us begin this journey together, one chapter at a time! Good luck!

CHAPTER ONE

WHY USE QUICKBOOKS?

Self-Employed

Managing your accounts, along with understanding and following your taxes, can be an especially difficult task if you are a self-employed individual. It can prove to be nerve-wracking and time-consuming, even if you are an expert at these two things. For many, this happens because you can't divide your work with other people, and you are forced to do everything on your own. While being self-employed is a great way to achieve success while being your own boss, it can be quite problematic as well, especially when you are bombarded by tasks from all directions. But don't worry, QuickBooks can help you solve at least a couple of problems. That way, you will have ample free time to deal with others. QuickBooks is a great bookkeeping software that can help you on the go!

QuickBooks is best suited for self-employed individuals as it is simple to use and is quite effective as well. The best thing about QuickBooks is that it is available in two versions - desktop and mobile. You create invoices, employee records, and various other key items using QuickBooks. Along with this, you can also reconcile bank accounts, record payments, and create details versions of loss and profit reports as well. All of this can be done using a single interface.

There are a variety of reasons why you, as a self-employed individual, should use QuickBooks Self-Employed. Let us have a look at them one by one.

It allows you to divide expenses between personal and business.

There are many business accounting software packages available on the market, but most of them only allow users to sync credit cards, bank accounts, and payment accounts. This way, many freelancers, who are generally self-employed, cannot divide their business expenses, which are often on the edge of personal and professional expenses. These expenses include Internet service, phones, texting services, etc. What makes QuickBooks special is that you can flag items as business or personal. You can also flag them as split.

While personal and business options are great, the split option is highly useful for self-employed people. It allows you to split the expenses on the basis of the percentage of the total transaction, or the dollar amount as well. It is also possible to set up split transactions that are generally used for personal or professional requirements. These expenses will be filtered automatically. This way, you will not miss any deductions.

Ease of Use

While all versions of QuickBooks are easy to use, the Self-Employed version makes it extremely easy to make rules on the basis of payments and purchases. It is quite simple to link your bank account to QuickBooks.

It is possible to review a list of transactions and then flag them as split, personal, or business. While flagging, you can also make rules for revenues and expenses simultaneously. These rules are generally created around vendor or client names. Thus, this method will perhaps be useless for people who get paid by personal cheques. For such transactions, you will have to choose the categories manually. While this method may not work for 'side-jobs,' it is great for ongoing revenues. This will make the whole process smooth and timesaving.

One of the best things about QuickBooks is that you do not need to use any form of coding to create rules. Rules can be created by simple menus and point and click operation. Thus, the learning curve for QuickBooks is extremely easy.

Tax Prediction

One of the biggest problems that freelancers generally face is how to calculate taxes. For a self-employed person calculating and managing taxes is not only frustrating but also a time-consuming task. But it is unavoidable as well. QuickBooks can help you save a lot of time by calculating and estimating taxes for you.

Whenever the user tags a transaction as a business transaction, QuickBooks automatically calculates and predicts the tax owned. This number is displayed all the time on the dynamic dashboard in the software. This can help you to save a lot of time and patience. You can use this saved time in any other important activity or your business. It also allows you to plan the payments and taxes efficiently.

The only problem with this method is that you cannot flag deposit transactions as business transactions if the taxes have been removed already. If you try to do this, the prediction will become messed up. In simple terms, if you label something as a business deposit, the mechanism will think that you have not paid any taxes.

This can be a problem for many self-employed people and freelancers where often the taxes are cut from the income and also at places where the taxes are deducted from the income already. But this does not mean that the function is totally useless - rather, it has many uses. You just need to find out how to utilize them for your own benefits while avoiding any misinformed decisions.

Impeccable Design

One of the best things about QuickBooks is the dashboard design. It is pretty and extremely well made. It does not look cheap or complicated. It is quite user-friendly and aesthetically pleasing as well. Its clean design is best for users who are not accustomed to the workings of bookkeeping software. It is easy to navigate and use. The main menu, which is present at the top left corner of the window allows you to access a variety of options, including Transactions, Home, Miles (used to record mileage), Reports, Taxes, and Invoices.

Another great innovation present on the dashboard is the snapshot option. In this option, all the menus present in the Main Menu are available as well. Along with the above options, there are also other options, including Loss, Profit, Accounts, Expenses, and Estimated Due Taxes.

Along with the above options, a to-do list is available as well. In this to-do list, there are multiple things, including recent transactions, additional tax information, etc.

Another great aspect about this software is that it can be easily synced with TurboTax. It also has a Tax Checklist, which is time-sensitive. This way, you will never have to wait for an accountant to put in your taxes until the last minute. This will make your life hassle-free.

Online Invoices and Payments

One of the most boring and tedious jobs regarding freelancing is tracking the progress of payment of different invoices. QuickBooks can help you avoid this problem efficiently. Using this software, you can issue invoices directly from the software itself. Similarly, you can also set and change due dates and process payments accordingly. If you do choose to make payments online, then you can also enable other options such as account transfers and credit card payments. It is also possible to use both of these options together. The receipts of these invoices will be directly sent to your email so that you can check them any time you want.

Whenever an invoice is not flagged as paid, and the due date for the invoice has passed, the software will automatically calculate it as an overdue invoice. This will be displayed on the dashboard and the main Invoice tab as well. You can choose to either resend the invoice, or you can also follow up with the client.

Managing Transactions in QuickBooks

QuickBooks Self-Employed is great and easy to use the cash-based system. In this system, you need to enter all the expenses and the payments that you receive, manually. This may sound like a difficult and time-consuming job, but it really is not. It is simple as adding transactions does not take more than a couple of seconds. It is also possible to add transactions by scanning or uploading receipts and invoices.

Adding transactions in this app is easy. You just need to click on the "Transactions" link present on the left of your window. Next, select "Add Transactions" on the top right. Next, select the type of transaction. This will mostly be business income or business expenses. Once this is done, you need to enter the total, description, and the category of the transaction. A long list of categories is available to keep your records clean and accessible.

Once the record has been saved, the total income will appear on the home page immediately. The profit and loss amounts will be updated as well.

Tracking Mileage

A very important concept related to business and finance is mileage. Mileage is a crucial, tax-deductible expense. It is rarely recorded in the proper way. If you fail to claim the proper transport expenses for your business, you will perhaps pay more tax than necessary. QuickBooks Self-Employed can help you in this case as it makes the whole process extremely easy.

You can enter your business trips with ease using the desktop version of the software, or you can also use the mobile app for the same task. The only thing that you need to do is to enter the proper start and end address. Your app will calculate the miles traveled automatically, and then based on your tax profile, will then calculate the deductible mileage expenses.

If you find this too time-consuming, you can also use the automatic mileage tracking option. This option is available in the mobile app. To use this, just start your mobile app when you are about to begin your journey. When you start your journey, just swipe and continue to drive. Stop the app once you reach your destination. The app will automatically calculate the number of miles of your travel and will show the same in your account. Thus, this method will not only save you a lot of time but will prevent a lot of unnecessary frustration as well.

QuickBooks and Taxation

Another great thing about QuickBooks is that it enables you to create your tax profile with ease. It features al the required information that is necessary for the calculation of your annual tax bill. For instance, in the United Kingdom, you need to enter your marital status and your personal tax-free allowance as well. The summary page will display all the necessary expenses and income. It will also show your tax liabilities at the end of the page. These are the only things that are generally required to file an online tax return.

Reporting

The report feature of the software is great as it not only provides you a simple tax summary, but it also has a list of all your current tax details. It is necessary to keep your tax data up to date and correct. If the information is not updated, the calculation of tax liabilities may go haywire.

You will also find the 'Profit and Loss' option in this section. The 'Profit and Loss' report is a complete analysis of your expenses, income, liabilities, assets, and profit. It is possible to view the reports of the current tax year and the previous tax year in many different options. For instance, you can view the reports by month, by year, or by quarters as well. The expenses are generally present at the bottom of the page, while your income and turnover are reported at the top. Your taxable profit is present under the 'Net Income' section.

Handling Invoices inside QuickBooks

QuickBooks Self-Employed has an in-depth invoice section that is great for keeping track of your payments and bills. You can keep track of the bills that have been paid and those that have not been paid. It is necessary to understand that the settled invoices are not carried forward to the tax summary and profit and loss report on its own. If you mark your invoice as 'Paid,' you will still have to create a transaction for the amount to avoid causing problems.

Creating an invoice in this software is easy. Just click on the 'Create invoice' option, which is present at the top of the screen. A box named 'Client name' will be visible. If the client is a new one, which means that you have never invoiced him or her before, then it is necessary to input his or her details. These details include full name, contact details such as phone number, and email address. If you plan to send the invoice to an old (or existing) client, then the details will be filled automatically.

Once the client has been added, you need to 'Add work.' In this box, you need to enter a few details regarding the nature of the job. A small description will suffice. You will be presented with an option to choose either an hourly rate or a flat rate. Next, enter a cash value and then finally press 'Add to invoice.' In the relevant box, add the preferred payment details and then click 'Send invoice,' which will be present at the bottom of your page. It is recommended to check the invoice once again before sending it. You can also save the invoice as a draft for future use.

Once you receive the payment of the invoice, go to the invoice page again and click "Mark paid." The color of the link will turn green from gray. This will indicate that you have successfully finished the transaction.

Self-employment is indeed great as it allows you to enjoy things at your own pace. But managing accounts can be a difficult task, which is why you should use QuickBooks to solve all your problems.

Being self-employed doesn't leave too much spare time for admin and accounts. But you can make things a lot easier for yourself by using a comprehensive accounting software package such as QuickBooks.

Thus, it is clear that QuickBooks is a great product for self-employed people and freelancers. It is affordable and cost-effective. It is great for people who want to take their business to the next level and become more successful. It is a great, all-in-one choice that will solve all your accounting problems. If you ever need more functions, you can always move on to the next version.

CHAPTER TWO

OPERATING QUICKBOOKS

QuickBooks is a simple, easy to use, a small business accounting program that can be used to manage expenses, costs, sales, and can be used to keep track of day-to-day transactions as well. It can be used to pay bills, invoice customers, file taxes, generate plans and reports, etc. There are various iterations available for QuickBooks, which have a variety of features according to the needs and requirements of business owners.

As there are a variety of QuickBooks options available, it can sometimes seem to be a bit daunting. It is recommended to understand it thoroughly before using it. You should test all the bells and whistles of the program. This way, you will understand how the basics of the program, and you will not find it difficult to use.

What Tasks do Small Businesses Use QuickBooks For?

Generally, small business owners prefer to use QuickBooks to check their invoices, keep an understanding of their cash flows, and pay their expenses. Some business owners also tend to utilize it to generate monthly and annual financial reports. It can also be used to prepare annual and quarterly business taxes as well. Many people generally use QuickBooks themselves, but some small business owners also prefer to use in-house bookkeepers as well.

Manage Sales and Income

You can check your income and sales using QuickBooks. This can be done by creating new invoices to track customer sales. It is recommended to use this function to keep in mind what your customers owe to you. This can be done if you know how to review your Accounts Receivable Aging Report. In this report, you can find the details about your current as well as old due invoices.

Check Expenses and Bills

QuickBooks can also be used to keep track of your bills along with expenses by connecting them directly to your bank, as well as a credit card account. This way, QuickBooks can keep track of your expenses by downloading them automatically and categorizing them as well. You can track cash transactions as well as check and record them in the QuickBooks in no time.

QuickBooks can also help you to pay bills before the due date. For instance, you can create an Accounts Payable Report, which will ensure that all your bills get paid on time. This report is great as it will allow having a look at all your current as well as past bills. This is great for troubleshooting if a problem arises in the future.

Reporting Insights

You can use QuickBooks to manage your cash inflow as well as outflow activities with ease. Due to this option, you can gain important insight related to your business efficiently. The reports are pre-built in QuickBooks. These reports can be accessed in a few simple clicks. These reports are updated automatically in real-time whenever you enter or save transactions.

This is especially great if you need to display your financials to a would-be investor or if you want to show them to your lender.

Along with the above-mentioned Accounts Receivable Report as well as the Accounts Payable Report, you can also have the following three reports to understand the health of your business. These reports are:

- Profit and Loss Report

- Balance Sheet Report

- Statement of Cash Flows

Let us have a look at these three reports one by one:

Profit and Loss Report

The profit and loss report can be created quickly. In this report, you can check how profitable you are as it contains a summary of your income from which your expenses are subtracted. It thus displays your bottom-line net income for a stipulated period; a week, a month, or even a quarter

Balance Sheet Report

The second report that can be used to study the health of your business is the Balance Sheet Report. In this report, you can check Liabilities, Assets, and Equity for your business at any specific point. You can create a balance sheet report in no time.

Statement of Cash Flow

The third report that you can create to check the health of your business is the Statement of Cash Flow. In this report, you can check the activities that affect your financing, investing, and operations of cash inflow as well as cash outflow.

Run Payroll

Payroll is a crucial aspect of any financial firm. You should avoid making any errors or mistakes in this section. If you make any mistakes while calculating a paycheck, it can lead to a lot of problems, including unhappy employees and high penalties as well. To solve this, QuickBooks has its own payroll option, which can calculate and run payroll automatically whenever you need it.

The QuickBooks payroll option is integrated with QuickBooks; this way, all your financial statements remain up to date all the time. It is recommended to buy QuickBooks payroll subscription so that you can utilize the payroll functions with ease.

Here is a small list of all the pros of using the payroll functions of QuickBooks:

- It can calculate the state as well as federal payroll taxes automatically

- You can pay employees with direct deposits or checks as well

- The program fills your tax forms automatically

- You can e-pay using QuickBooks

Track Inventory

You can use QuickBooks to keep track of your inventory as well. You can input details such as unit costs and on-hand amounts. QuickBooks will automatically track and update the details for you according to the transactions. In QuickBooks, there is a multitude of options that can be used to manage the inventory.

Tracking your inventory in an Excel sheet can take a lot of time and effort. But you can save these efforts and time by using QuickBooks.

Simplification of Taxes

QuickBooks can help you simplify your taxes significantly. You do not need to put a lot of time and effort into this. Taxes take a lot of time. It does not matter if you have all the receipts or if you have been tracking them meticulously in a spreadsheet file, ultimately, it will take you a lot of effort to file your tax returns.

QuickBooks can simplify this process a great deal. You can manage your business accounts and taxes using QuickBooks. You just need to set up your tax professional and allow him or her to access your QuickBooks data to collect information that is required to file tax returns. QuickBooks tracks everything meticulously, which is why you do not need to waste time organizing bank statements and receipts. This makes the whole process accurate, timesaving, and effortless as well.

Accept Online Payments

To make cash flow quick, efficient, and user-friendly, you should allow your customers to pay your invoices online. This can be quite difficult to manage, but you can do it with ease using QuickBooks. It is possible to add the Intuit Payments feature to your QuickBooks to enable online payment options with just a simple click of a button.

Once this option is activated, you can send invoices using email. All your emails will now have a "Pay Now" button as well. Whenever you send an invoice to a customer, he or she will be able to click the button and pay the invoice using their bank account or using any major credit cards they may have. This makes transactions hassle-free.

You do not need to pay any sort of monthly fee to use this option. You just need to pay the following charges:

- Bank Transfers (ACH) – Free

- Card Invoiced – 2.9% plus 25 cents

- Card Swiped – 2.4% plus 25 cents

- Card Keyed-in – 3.4% plus 25 cents

Scan Receipts

QuickBooks also allows you to scan your receipts, which makes the tax procedures effortless. If you are using QuickBooks Online, you can download the QuickBooks app on your mobile phones for free. Once you have downloaded the app, you can take pictures of the receipts and upload them to QuickBooks Online in no time.

Scanning the receipts and uploading them to QuickBooks Online will make your life stress-free. You will no longer have to worry about keeping and manually matching receipts. Similarly, you will never lose receipts anymore. You can upload any number of receipts to QuickBooks Online. This option is especially great for businesses that need to keep track of a lot of expenses, including law firms, lawyers, doctors, etc.

QuickBooks Features & Pricing

As said above, there are many different versions of QuickBooks available on the market. All of them have a variety of functions and options. These options change according to the need and requirements of the users. Before buying a QuickBooks version, it is recommended to have a look at different options and check that suits your needs the most. Let us have a look at the options in brief.

QuickBooks Online

This is one of the most used versions of QuickBooks as it does not require any kind of software installation, and it can be used from anywhere, as all the data is stored in the cloud. This version is available in three different versions, which are Simple, Essential, and Plus. It is highly recommended for all service-based firms and businesses that do not use complicated invoices. You can access the data stored on QuickBooks Online from any computer if you have the login details and an Internet connection.

QuickBooks Desktop

Like QuickBooks Online, QuickBooks Desktop comes in three different versions. These are Pro, Premier, and Enterprise. Unlike QuickBooks Online, you need to install software on your computer to use this version. This version is great for small businesses that are not into manufacturing. It is great for retailers, non-profit businesses, contractors, etc. The Enterprise version of the QuickBooks Desktop, as the name suggests, is best for large enterprises. This version is often considered to be industry-specific as it features reports and custom chart of accounts for the company.

QuickBooks Self-Employed

Nowadays the number of people who are either self-employed or are freelancers has increased significantly. QuickBooks has an option for such people as well. QuickBooks Self-Employed is a great product for freelancers, contractors, self-employed people, Lyft or Uber drivers, and real estate agents. It is based on the cloud-like QuickBooks Online. You can access this version from any computer if you have the login details and an Internet connection. The best thing about this version is that it has a multitude of features that are not present in any other version of QuickBooks. These features include the option to keep personal and business expenses separate, to transfer data to TurboTax, and to track miles as well.

It can also calculate and estimate your tax payments and can also remind you whenever they are due.

QuickBooks Mac

QuickBooks Mac, as the name suggests, is the only desktop version available for Mac users. If you do not want to use QuickBooks Online, then you can use this version if you have a Mac computer. This product is quite similar to the QuickBooks Pro. It is suitable for small businesses and firms that are not into manufacturing.

CHAPTER THREE

PAYROLL

Payroll is essential for business owners if you want to save money, pay your employees properly, and manage your taxes. Setting up and running payroll is extremely easy if you use QuickBooks Online. In this chapter, let us have a look at the data that is required to set up a payroll. Then, let us have a look at the steps involved to run a payroll.

Adding the Intuit Payroll to your already present QuickBooks account can help your business grow exponentially. You will be able to reap a multitude of benefits such as same-day deposits, taxes, help in setting up payroll, etc. This makes it a great investment for any business.

Payroll Setup: Data that you need

Before running payroll in QuickBooks, you need to set it up in the QuickBooks Online version. This is a simple process that does not take a lot of effort or time. Before moving on to the step-by-step instructions regarding payroll set up, it is necessary to have a look at some documents that are absolutely necessary for setting it up. Here is a list of all the documents that you need to set up a payroll.

Add Employer Information

Before setting up your payroll account, you need to have a business bank account and the routing number of the account. This account will be used to make tax payments and to pay the employees as well. Along with this, you need to have the salary information or the hourly rate of the employees as well. You should also be aware of other perks, including health insurance, retirement plans, incentives, etc. Here is a list of things that you must have:

Bank Account Information

You must have the account number and the routing number of the checking account from which you are going to write a check for the employees. This account is also used for making tax payments. (It is recommended to have a payroll account that will be different from your checking account that will be used for your daily business.

Employee Compensation

Under this section, you need to add the salaries, the hourly rates, tips, commissions, bonuses, and anything else that you give to your employees.

Employee Benefits

In this section, add any benefits that you provide to your employees. These include 401, dental insurance, health insurance, vacation policies, retirement policies, sick leave policy, and FSA or Flexible Spending Account.

Other

In this section, include anything else that is relevant. This section generally includes mileage reimbursement, cash advances, wage garnishments, union dues, etc.

Add Employee Info

QuickBooks cannot calculate payroll checks efficiently if you do not feed employee data in it. You need to have a variety of data, including Form W-4, deductions, pay rate, frequency of pay, etc.

Here is a small list of data that you need to enter in QuickBooks to successfully run a payroll:

Form W-4

When a firm or business hires a new employee, the employee needs to fill a form called Form W-4. In this form, the employee needs to add all withholding data along with any other important and pertinent information that is required to calculate the payroll tax deductions.

Pay Rate

This is the hourly rate or the salary that you pay employees. This section should also include any commission or bonus that you pay to employees (if applicable).

Paycheck Deductions

In this section, you need to add the employees' role in their retirement plans, health insurance, dental insurance, and garnishments.

Pay Schedule

In this section, you need to add the pay schedule of the employees. Generally, it is supposed to be weekly, twice a week, twice a month, or monthly. QuickBooks also offers you a flexible payment schedule. For instance, you also pay hourly employees every week, while salaried employees once a month, etc. Both of these pay schedules can be set up simultaneously.

Vacation or Sick Hours Policy

Generally, firms offer vacation or sick pay. For this, you need to input the information of all the employees. Generally, these hours are gained at the end of each pay period.

Hire Date

In this section, you need to enter the hiring date for each employee carefully.

Direct Deposit Authorization Form

In this section, you need to offer your employees the option of direct deposit as an alternative to check. To do this, you need to file the direct deposit authorization form. This will provide you with permission to make deposits into your employees' accounts. It will also allow you to rout the data required to make such deposits.

Doing payroll in QuickBooks is easy. In this section, let us have a look at the steps required to set up payroll in QuickBooks.

How to Set Up QuickBooks Payroll

In this section, let us have a look at the QuickBooks enhanced payroll service. Here is a list of steps that you need to undertake to run a payroll in QuickBooks Online successfully.

Go to the Employee Center

To begin the payroll process, you need to first click on the Employees tab, which is present on the left menu bar. A new window will open.

Payroll Setup

If you have bought the payroll service with QuickBooks Online subscription, then a window will appear on your screen. In this window, click on the "Get Set Up" button. A new window will appear. If you have not subscribed for payroll option yet, then you need to click on "Add Payroll." Once you have added payroll, you can click on the "Get Set Up" button.

Respond to the Questions

In the next window, you need to add some information. This is essential because you need to provide additional information to make the process smooth. This information is also required to make your W-2 forms accurate. To do this, you need to provide data related to any payrolls that you have issued during the year.

Add Employees

Once the above step is done, you can start adding employees to the program. To do so, just click on "Add an Employee." A new window will appear.

Complete Employee Info

In this step, you need to add the relevant and important information related to employees one by one.

Here is a list of all the fields that you need to fill in to run payroll successfully:

Employee Withholding Information

This data can be generally found in the Form W-4. To edit this section, just click on the Pencil icon.

Pay Schedule

To add this, just click on the 'Pay Schedule' option from the drop-down menu. There are a variety of options available in this section, including weekly, monthly, bimonthly, etc.

Employee Pay

As the name suggests, you need to enter the wages of the employees in this section. You can add different kinds of payment types in this section. To do so, just click on the 'Add Additional Pay Types' link, which is present under this field.

Employee Contribution/Deduction

In this section, you need to add the contributions or the deductions for the employees.

Payment Method

In this section, you need to select the mode of payment from the drop-down menu. Here you need to select from live check or direct deposit. If you choose direct deposit, then you need to input the bank details of the employee.

Year to Date Payroll

In this section, you need to enter last year's payroll information of the employee.

Finishing all these fields is essential, as it will reflect on your payroll system. It is required to fill the pertinent information of all the employees carefully. It is also recommended to double-check the data to avoid any mistakes. If you commit any errors here, your payroll calculations will turn out wrong as well.

How to Run Payroll in QuickBooks Online

In the last section, we saw how to set up your employees. In this section, let us have a look at how to run your payroll. In this section, you will learn how to input your payroll hours and other data using which your program will calculate the payroll checks and the payroll taxes automatically. You can then either print and pay the checks, or you can deposit them directly to the employees.

Let us have a look at the steps required to run payroll in QuickBooks Online.

Go to the Employee Center

Once again, go to the Employees tab situated on the left menu bar. A new window will open.

Click "Run Payroll"

In the new dashboard, you will see a list of employees that you set up using the steps given in the last section. Check the list and then click on the 'Run payroll' button situated in the top right corner.

Enter Current Payroll Hours

In the next screen, enter the total hours worked for hourly employees. Double-check other information. To enter hours as well as rates in the payrolls option, you need to fill in the following fields:

Bank Account

In this, you need to enter the details of the bank account from which the taxes and payroll checks are going to be deducted. If the bank details are incorrect, then change them from the drop-down menu.

Pay Period

In this section, you need to check the pay periods that you have entered in the last tutorial. If they are not correct, rectify them using the drop-down menu.

Pay Date

In this section, you need to check the date of payment for your employees.

Hours Worked

In this section, you need to enter the hours for which the employees have worked. (Only in the case of hourly employees.)

Salary Employees

Here, the program will calculate the annual salary automatically. Just crosscheck it once to ensure that it is correct.

Total Pay

In this section, the gross total of the pays of all the employees present on payroll will be given.

Review & Submit Payroll

In this step, you are supposed to check and review the data once again before finalizing it. If you believe that everything is accurate, you can move on; if not, go back and rectify the errors. Once you are satisfied with the details, click on the Submit button at the bottom of the page. Use the on-screen directions to either print the checks or the print the direct deposit slips.

Congratulations! You have successfully run your first payroll using QuickBooks.

CHAPTER FOUR

TRACKING RECEIPTS

Businesses and enterprises do not work on goodwill. You need to be meticulous and disciplined when running a business. If you are not disciplined or are too careless, you will never earn profit from your business. It is necessary to keep track of all the receipts that are collected while doing business. In this chapter, let us have a close look at receipts and how they are tracked.

Sales receipts are essential if you want to conduct your business successfully. Normally, if you work in retail, sales receipts are a must. You cannot function without sales receipts. It is necessary to pay close attention to sales receipts when you run an enterprise. It is required to take them seriously. These receipts contain crucial data, and they reflect the methods of your business accounting. Sometimes managing and creating these receipts can be a difficult and time-consuming task, but you can do it with ease using QuickBooks.

What Is a Sales Receipt?

Before moving on to the role of QuickBooks in the management of sales receipts, it is necessary to understand what sales receipts are. In simple terms, sales receipts are documents that show a sale. This document is essential as it acknowledges that the seller has paid for either services or goods. The receipt is given to the buyer by the seller.

Receipts are only provided once the service or the goods have been given to the customer. Generally, the customer needs to pay for these goods or services in full. In some cases, some businesses also issue partial receipts. This generally happens when a customer buys a costly or high-priced product and pays for it with the help of installments. Partial receipts are also issued when the seller offers a king of continuous service to the customer, and the customer pays the seller on a recurring basis as well. In such cases, the sales receipt generally shows the remaining balance as well.

What Information should be present on a Sales Receipt?

A variety of receipts are available in the world of finance. Generally, a seller designs the receipt according to his or her business. He or she can add anything he or she wants on the receipt, but there are certain things that need to be on the receipt, or it becomes useless.

Here is a small list of items that should be present on the receipt:

- The name of the product or service

- The UPC of the service or the product

- The quantity of the service or the product

- The sale price of the service or the product

- The total amount of the sale

- The rate of sales tax

- The amount of tax

- The total price of the tax

In the case of tax, it is necessary to create correct and complete receipts. If the receipts are inaccurate, then the tax calculation will be erroneous.

To make a receipt more useful, it is recommended to add the following details on your receipt.

- The GST registration number of the seller

- The date, address, and time of the sale

- The name of the business

- The contact information of the business. This includes email address, phone number, or website.

- The name of the sales associate who did the business

- Along with these, you can also add the following items to your receipt:

- Customer information including name and contact number

- Company logo

- Branding material

- Coupons

- Marketing copy

What are Gift Receipts?

Almost all receipts carry a standard amount of data, but there are certain receipts like gift receipts that are different from regular receipts. Gift receipts contain some pertinent information regarding the sale, but they generally do not contain the price of the product or service. This way, the recipient can give or take the product or the service without seeing the price. Certain gift receipts include the name of the products, but most of them only have a barcode that can be scanned by business people only. This is used to access the sales record of the particular product.

It solely depends on the seller whether the gift receipt will be held valid for returns or not. Generally, it is only valid for exchanges. Certain customers tend to ask for custom gift receipts as well. It is recommended to clarify the return and exchange policies to such customers to avoid any further nuisance.

The Importance of Receipts

Receipts are extremely crucial as they are the official sales records for your firm. It is necessary to safeguard them and manage them carefully. It is also necessary to create them correctly. Inaccurate receipts can lead to a lot of problems internally as well as externally. Internally, the receipts are used to track your sales and the amounts that you gain. This means that they can be used to calculate the cash flow, the profit statement, and the loss statement as well. This information is essential as it allows you to make proper and better business decisions. It can also help you to make and understand long-term plans.

Externally, receipts are important because they are used for tax filing. As a business, it is your duty to record your sales as well as the tax that you charge your buyers. This information is crucial as it helps you to file and pay taxes properly. Without this information, you will not be able to pay taxes correctly. Sometimes you need to create a paper trail that can help you to prove your tax number and sales int eh case of an audit.

Detailed receipts are also important and useful for your buyers as well. They can help them to prove deductible expenses, record paid taxes, and track business costs as well. Thus, when they file taxes, the receipts can help them a lot.

What's the Difference between an Invoice and a Sales Receipt?

Invoices and sales receipts often seem to be similar, which is why people often confuse them. It is true that both of them are used to record sales and contain almost the same information. But they are still different. The differences lie in how they are used in accounting and how they are issued.

Generally, a receipt is the record of a sale that has been completed. It is normally issued after payment. For instance, if a customer bought B number of products at C price, got the products, and paid the total C price, then the customer will get a receipt. This is because the seller will have the money in his or her hand, and there will no further exchange or transaction of any sort. This sale will be written as income in your books. You can further deposit this amount in your bank. Unless the customer comes back for a return or refund, the sale is finished.

Invoices generally record an unfinished or partial transaction. They are generally issued before the payment is made. They are used to track the sale. Invoices are usually used in the service industry more than in the retail industry. For instance, when a homeowner signs a painter to paint his or her house, both parties agree on a price. The painter will then issue an invoice to the homeowner containing details such as records of the services that are to be done, the price of the service, and the date when it will be completed. Once the service gets done, the homeowner will clear the invoice and will get a receipt from the painter, who will denote that the transaction is done. Invoices are also used in the case of electricity bills, phone bills, and credit card statements as well.

Sometimes retail stores to issue invoices to buyers. Invoices are generally issued to customers who have credit accounts — this way, the customer can receive the product first and pay the price later.

As said above, invoices are recorded in a different way as compared to regular sales receipts. Companies generally consider invoices as receivables and not as income. This way, they understand that the sale is not complete and that it will be complete in the future. The sale or the amount can only be recorded as 'income' when the sale is complete and when the amount is deposited in the bank account.

Different Receipt Types for Different Industries

There exists no typical or standard format of receipt. Different companies and industries have different forms of receipts. But sometimes, certain forms become standard, unofficially. Here is a small list of different kinds of sales receipts that are generally used around the world. It needs to be understood that these are not hard and fast forms, and they change according to the industry and the needs and requirements of the seller.

Register Tape

This is a common form of receipt that is generally used in transactions where the customer comes face to face with the seller. The receipt is printed automatically and can be torn off instantaneously. It is great for companies that deal with high volume sales. These receipts are generally used in grocery stores, gas stations, and specialty shops as well.

Handwritten Carbons

This is another form of receipt that is often used in impromptu sales as well as the personal-service industry. For instance, landlords often use this method to acknowledge rent payment. These receipts are also used by businessmen who conduct their business out of temporary stalls or makeshift locations. These stalls are generally present at conventions, trade shows, etc.

Contractors who try to find new business in their respective fields such as roofing contractors, gardeners, landscapers, etc. who are supposed to visit the houses of customers generally use these receipts as well.

At the end of the week, you can collect and input the data collected from these receipts in your accounting system. Handwritten receipts are accepted in many states if they do not appear suspicious.

Invoices

These are extremely common in business-to-business records. Many buyers tend to ask for invoices in a specific manner for their own bookkeeping purposes. Invoices are generally printed and mailed or handed over, but nowadays, a lot of people send them online as well. Certain online payment processors can create an invoice according to the request of the payment. QuickBooks Online is better than such options as it allows you to create custom invoices according to the requirement of the customer. You can also set up a general format that can be used for all the other customers.

Packing Slips

These receipts are generally used by enterprises that deal with shipping. Such companies only ship the items to the customers and do not sell them in person. The packing slips contain a complete detailed list of all the items that have been shipped to you along with the prices of the items and the contact details of the company. Certain companies also include return labels as well. This slip is generally present in your delivery.

As said above, there are a variety of sales receipts that change according to the needs and requirements of the sellers, and in some cases, the customers as well.

How to Make a Sales Receipt

A variety of options are available to make your own small business receipts. These options depend on your needs, your requirements, the nature of your business, the level of personalization, the details that you want to use, and affordability. Your sales receipts and the information present on your receipts communicate your ideas to customers. Good receipts can help you bring in future customers who will feel comfortable dealing with you.

Generally, companies that use field sales associates tend to use handwritten receipts. These receipts are convenient options for such companies. While it is true that these receipts take a lot of time to be filled, they offer a lot of flexibility as well. This is because they are blank canvases in which you can input the data according to your requirements.

If you decide to use handwritten sales receipts, it is recommended to find pre-printed templates that will be suitable for your industry or business. For instance, if you have a landscaping business, it is recommended to find a blank template where details such as yard size, grass type, plants, etc. are mentioned. It should also have some details related to edging, fences, weeding, etc. Similarly, if you own a marketing business, your blank template should have details such as the number of hours, description of the service, the hourly rate, etc. If you are a new business, it is recommended to use handwritten receipts as they are not only easy to use, but they also offer you ample opportunity to refine and grow your business. Most handwritten receipts generally need only a receipt pad and pen. This makes them extremely cost-effective and efficient. It is recommended to make some stamps to make writing receipts effortless.

If you are a new company and you need occasional receipts, then you can make receipts on simple word processors such as LibreOffice or Microsoft Word as well. Most of these programs generally have inbuilt receipt templates that can be edited and customized according to the needs, requirements, and nature of your business. If you cannot find a decent receipt template, you can download a new one at affordable rates.

You can also design your own template from scratch. This option is best for users who like to have personalized and highly customized receipts. It is recommended to use tables in your receipt to make it easy to read and track. Tables will also help you to keep everything organized. It is recommended to highlight important details such as the name of the customer, the tax, the total, the grand total, the subtotal, etc. This option allows you to add anything you want to your receipt, including add-on services, ID numbers, details, etc.

Word Processors are also great if you run a shipping business. If you do not retail a lot of products, you can create manual receipts in word processors. If you make a lot of deals every day, then you can also link your sales database to the document. This way, the document will take all the relevant data automatically and save you a lot of time and effort. You can then print these receipts and put them in the shipment. It is easy to create PDFs using word processors, which makes emailing receipts a piece of cake.

While these methods are great if you have a small business where you have a lot of time to manage things, these methods can be quite time consuming if you have a large business. In the case of large businesses, it is recommended to use some dedicated receipt software, such as QuickBooks.

Creating Sales Receipts in QuickBooks Online

QuickBooks is a great program that can help you to create and email sales receipts from a desktop computer efficiently. If you have the QuickBooks Online version, then you can create and send sales receipts from any device that is connected to the Internet. So if your employees are on the field and want to create invoices on their tablets or phones, they can do so with ease. This intuitive and easy to use feature helps you to customize receipts according to the nature of your company. You can personalize your receipts according to your requirements.

It is extremely simple to create receipts in QuickBooks. It is also timesaving and takes merely a few moments to do so. When you open and sign in to QuickBooks account, just click the plus sign. Next, click on the Customers menu. Here, click on the Choose Sales

Receipt, and a blank window will be presented on the screen. In the blank form, you input the necessary details that are pertinent to the sales receipt. This normally includes business name, customer's name, contact details, etc. If the customer is new, you can also save him or her as a frequent customer to avoid entering these details every time.

Once you have entered the name or the customer, add the items or the service that you sold. If you have a set of items that you sell, you can save these items in the inventory list so that you do not have to add the items every time you make a sales receipt. If you sell miscellaneous items, then avoid making inventories. Try to find other timesaving options and methods that will work for you.

Adding new items in QuickBooks is quick and easy. You can add a variety of details such as the name of the product, information related to the product, the ID number, or the description of the product as well. Once these details have been added, add the per-unit price for the product. You do not need to add the subtotal, as the program will calculate it with the help of prices and quantities of your products. QuickBooks knows your industry and location. This is essential because it can add the sales tax (if necessary) to the receipt automatically. If you ever want to change an item, remove it, or add it, or change the price of the item or update the quantity of the products, the total of the receipt will change as well. Another feature that makes QuickBooks really efficient is that you can add discounts and tips using the program.

Once the receipt becomes ready, you get a variety of options. You can preview the final version of the receipt using the Print Preview option. If you find any problems or errors, you can make changes immediately. Once you are satisfied with the receipt, you can then save it to the database. You can then either print the receipt or send it to the customer directly.

One of the best things about receipt generators like QuickBooks is that it can be integrated into the accounts system with ease. This way, your bookkeeping functions become easy and coherent. Whenever you make a receipt, you can flag it as an income account or as an account receivable. The funds will then automatically get transferred to your financial records. You will not have to input them in a separate manner.

If your company generally does a lot of repeat deals with different people, QuickBooks can help you save a lot of time and energy. Once you input the information of a customer in QuickBooks Online, the information gets saved on the cloud. Next time whenever you want to create a receipt, you can use the auto-fill option to fill the information in the receipt. Even if you do not make repeated deals with a customer, the saved information can still be useful. You can access the saved information any time and check the details of the transaction quickly. The best thing about storing information and sales record online is that it is almost impossible to lose the data. It is always safe and secure. It is easy to lose hard copies of sales receipts. But virtual sales receipts rarely get lost. These sales receipts also have time stamps. This way, you can create a virtual 'paper' trail that cannot be changed. This paper trail is great for tax purposes. This method is also great for your customers who can check the expenses whenever they want. Thus, this method is great for both the sellers as well as customers.

Managing Sales Receipts for Your Small Business

Sales receipts are essential if you are a small business owner. These receipts can be used to keep a record of your finances accurately. But to manage these receipts, it is necessary to have a good receipt management system as well. For instance, you must have seen some restaurants with metal spikes near registers where receipts are pierced and stacked. This method is great for keeping the receipts safe until the end of the day. At the end of the day, the receipts are removed and then added to the books. Many people also tend to use special receipt drawers and receipt boxes as well.

If you want to use a modern method to save your records, you can save the digital copies as well. This can be done by maintaining the copies of the transactions on the server of the devices present at the point of sale. You can then use this data to fill your spreadsheet to maintain your books. If you enable autofill, then this data will be filled automatically. It is quite similar to the metal spike method, but it is more time-efficient and does not need a lot of papers as well. Thus, it is environment-friendly as well.

But there are many other options to manage your receipts, especially if you do not want to wait until the end of the day to manage your books. For instance, QuickBooks and similar programs can help you save the data in real-time on the cloud. Due to this, you can check data and total after each sale. Cloud-based programs are great because they can also allow you to print register tape while the employees are still working. Even if your employees are out in the field and are working, you can print out sales projections with ease. Just allow your employees to add data in the program, and the program will do the necessary work for you immediately.

CHAPTER FIVE

INVENTORY

Tracking and keeping a record of your inventory can be a difficult job, but you need to do it correctly to avoid any problems in the future. There are many methods of tracking and managing your inventory. While managing your inventory by hand is a decent option if you do not have a lot of items for sale if you have a lot of items, then managing an inventory manually can be quite difficult.

There are a variety of QuickBooks options available for your perusal. You can use inventory options in QuickBooks Pro, QuickBooks Premier, and QuickBooks Enterprise edition as well. These features are generally disabled when you install these programs. You can enable the functions and can begin with tracking in no time. Once these functions are activated, you can manage inventory with ease. You will also get alerts whenever you need to reorder items or whenever you need to purchase new products. Using the QuickBooks inventory function is fairly easy, and you can start adding products to the inventory almost instantly.

Check Your Subscription First

Before beginning your inventory process, you need to check whether you are subscribed to the inventory option or not. If you are not subscribed to the function, then you will not be able to add entries in your inventory. Inventory management is not available with all the plans, so check whether you are subscribed to the inventory manager or not. To do this, open QuickBooks and click on the gear-shaped icon. This will open a menu. In this menu, select Accounts and Settings, and here click on Locate. Next, select the Billing and Subscription option. Here you can check your current plan. If you see that you are not subscribed to the Inventory function, then it is recommended to subscribe to it immediately to unlock the inventory-related features and functions in QuickBooks.

How to Set Up Inventory Parts and Non-Inventory Parts in QuickBooks

Once you confirm that you have subscribed to the inventory options in QuickBooks, it is time to add to the inventory.

It is possible to add both inventory and non-inventory items in the program. This is done for the reason of tracking. Inventory items are the items that are currently in stock. For instance, if you have a grocery business, then the number of certain cookies will be added to the inventory. Non-inventory items are the items that are not in stock but can be ordered specially on the request of customers.

To add inventory items to QuickBooks, you need to switch on the inventory tracking option. To add non-inventory parts, you do not need to change any settings. Let us now have a simple look at how to add items to inventory and non-inventory.

Inventory Parts

1. Open the QuickBooks program and click on 'Edit' from the menu bar.

2. In the Edit menu, choose 'Preferences.'

3. In this menu, click on 'Items and Inventory.'

4. Next, click on the 'Company Preferences' tab.

5. Check the box near 'Inventory and Purchase orders are active.' This will allow inventory tracking.

6. Click OK.

7. Click on 'Items and Services' in the Home window.

8. Click on the 'Item' button and then click on 'New.'

9. Click on 'Inventory Part' from the drop-down menu.

10. Input the name of the item in the 'Item Name/Number' box.

11. Click on the 'Income Account' drop-down menu. In this menu, choose the account that you would like to use to track the income of this inventory.

12. Add the remaining information and finally click 'OK.'

This will successfully create an inventory item.

Non-Inventory Parts

Adding non-inventory parts is easier than adding inventory parts. Let us have a look at the steps required to add non-inventory parts.

1. Click on the 'Items and Services' option in the Home window.

2. Click on the 'Item' button.

3. Click on the 'New' option to open a new item window.

4. Click on 'Non-inventory Part' from the drop-down menu.

5. Input the name of the item in the 'Item Name/Number' box.

6. Choose the account that you would like to link to the item using the drop-down menu.

7. Add any remaining and pertinent information and click 'OK.'

This will create a non-inventory item.

Set Up and Track your Inventory

Setting up and tracking your inventory is easy in QuickBooks. It has all the options that are necessary to set up and manage your inventory. You can track what you have in hand, receive notifications when things are running out, and check the records of what you purchase and sell. Here is a small tutorial of how to set up your inventory and get it running. These steps are easy to understand and follow.

Step 1: Turn on Inventory Tracking

If you have not turned on inventory tracking yet, you need to do so as soon as possible. These settings need to be turned on if you want to add things to your inventory. To start inventory tracking:

1. Go to the Settings option.

2. Click on Company Settings.

3. Click on Sales.

4. Click the Products and services section.

5. Click Edit.

6. Click on the Checkbox near Show Product/Service option.

7. Click on the Checkbox near the Track Quantity option.

8. Click on the Checkbox near Track inventory quantity on hand.

9. Click on Save.

10. Select Done.

Step 2: Add your Inventory Products

Once you have set up your inventory tracking, it is now time to add items to your inventory. It should be noted that all the things that you buy, or sell are not a part of your inventory. You also need to set up the following things in QuickBooks to make your inventory perfect:

Non-Inventory Items

As said above, these are the items that you buy and sell but do not have a stock of. These items generally involve custom order items. This listing also involves installation programs such as nuts, bolts, etc.

Services

In this section, you are supposed to add all the services that you provide to your customers. These include gardening, painting, landscaping, etc.

Bundles

In this section, you should create bundles of services or products that are sold together. For instance, gift baskets that include chocolates, flowers, and wine, etc. By adding these products as bundles, you can save a lot of time, as you won't have to add them individually in your invoice or receipt later.

Step 3: Keep Track of What Sells

Once you have successfully added and set up your inventory products, you need to track them according to their sales. There are two options available for tracking your sales, they are:

1. Create an invoice if you are going to receive the payment later.

2. Create a sales receipt if you receive the payment immediately.

QuickBooks can then reduce what's on hand as compared to the amount present on either the sales receipt or the invoice.

Check what's on hand and what's on order as you work.

Checking what is present in your store and what is still in the form of an invoice, receipt, or sales receipt is simple. Just move your mouse pointer over the quantity that you entered for a product. This will allow you to see more information regarding the product.

You can also set low stock alerts. QuickBooks will sell you a reminder to remind you that things are running low.

Step 4: Restock your Inventory

QuickBooks can automatically tell you whenever it is time to restock. It is possible to order inventory from the program itself. It will keep track of whatever is running low. Similarly, it will also keep track of things that you have ordered and received from the supplier. Once you receive the items, the quantity on hand will increase on its own as well.

Step 5: Use Reports to Check the Status of your Inventory

It is recommended to check the reports to check who the best-sellers are. You can also check the reports to learn about the price of the products, what products you currently have on hand, etc.

Negative Inventory

Negative inventory is a serious problem that can lead to grave errors later. In this section, let us have a look at what this problem is and how to solve it.

Negative Inventory Overview

Negative inventory is usually caused when you enter sales transactions before the corresponding purchase transactions have been entered. In simple words, it means that when you sell inventory items that are currently out of stock.

How to View Negative Inventory

There are different ways to check negative inventory. It generally appears on your Balance Sheet. It also appears on the following report:

IVD or Inventory Valuation Detail Report

The Inventory Valuation Detail Report or the IVD is the only report that can be used to understand the seriousness of your negative inventory. If you have negative inventory, it will show as negative numbers in the QOH or Quantity on Hand column.

To check whether you have a negative inventory problem or not:

1. Click on the Reports menu.

2. Click on Inventory.

3. Click on Inventory Valuation.

Negative Item Listing report

You can use the Negative Item Listing report function if you are using QuickBooks Enterprise 15.0 and later version. In this report, you view the current negative quantities, but this report will not display the past negative quantities.

To check whether you have a negative inventory problem or not:

1. Click on the Reports menu.

2. Click on Inventory.

3. Click on Negative Item Listing.

If you have the QuickBooks Enterprise 2014 version (or earlier) or the QuickBooks Premier version, you can check your negative inventory using Inventory Centre.

To check whether you have a negative inventory problem or not:

1. Click on the Suppliers menu.

2. Click on Inventory Activities.

3. Click on Inventory Center.

4. On the upper left corner of the Inventory Center window, change the filter form Active Inventory to Assembly, to QOH <=Zero.

How to Fix Negative Inventory Problem

In the last section, we saw what negative inventory problem is and how it arises. In this section, let us have a look at some of the methods that can be used to solve this problem.

Reminders

Before trying any of the below-mentioned methods to solve your inventory problem, it is necessary to follow these reminders. By keeping these things in mind, you will be able to avoid loss of data and, in general, frustration. These are simple tips that can be done without any efforts.

Back up your QuickBooks File. Do not overwrite any past backups. Keep all the backups safe and secure so that if you mess up, you can start with a backup once again.

Talk to your accounting professional to check whether the changes that you made are legitimate or not. Some people think that they can solve the negative inventory problem by adjusting the QOH or Quantity on Hand value from negative to positive. But this is false. You also need to change the negative QOH and take precautions to disallow it from happening again.

If you believe that the negative inventory problem is too serious and that it will take a lot of time and effort to repair it, then it is recommended to begin a new data file instead.

Let us now have a look at the variety of solutions that can help you solve the problem of negative inventory.

Your First Transaction for an Item in the Sale

Your inventory reports will turn out to be incorrect if you do no establish an average cost. To rectify this mistake, you need to assure that the earliest dated transaction of a product is a credit card charge, a check, a bill, or Adjust Qty/Value on Hand:

1. Click on the QuickBooks Reports menu.

2. Click on Inventory.

3. Click on the Inventory Valuation summary.

4. Use the QuickZoom function to focus on the item that is displaying wrong values. This can be done by double-clicking the name of the item.

5. A new window called the Inventory Valuation Detail Report will open.

6. QuickZoom on the first Bill.

7. In the new window, change the invoice date.

8. Click Save and close the bill.

9. Repeat these steps until you run out of items.

You sold inventory items without keeping records of the purchases.

Sometimes you may enter bills in the accounts but forget to add the inventory items. If this is the case, then just edit the Bills. To do so, you open the Expense Tab and change the entries. Do remember that changing these may change your inventory expenses as well. This is why it is recommended to consult your accounting professional before beginning this process.

You input purchases and/or adjustments before inputting sales.

If it is possible, change the transaction dates. The dates of the bills should be dated before the invoices.

To do so:

1. Click on the Menu bar and select Reports.

2. Select Inventory.

3. Select the Inventory Valuation Detail.

4. Click on the Dates drop-down menu.

5. Select All.

6. Check out the items to find the items that show the negative amount in the OHC or On Hand Column.

7. Change the dates of invoices.

8. Repeat until no negative entry is left.

How to prevent negative inventory

Preventing negative inventory problems is easy. Just remember not to sell inventory items until you buy them and enter them into QuickBooks.

1. Set up inventory items with an opening balance

2. Create a new inventory item.

3. Add all the necessary information.

4. At the end of the page, add QOH.

5. Also, add the Value. The program will calculate the average cost.

6. If you do not have any units on hand, it is recommended to input purchase before you input a sale.

Use Sales Orders to enter sales for which you do have inventory

To do so, you can either input the customer order as a Sales Order or as an Invoice. If you enter it as an Invoice, just mark the Invoice as Pending. You can do so from the Mark Invoice option from the Edit menu.

1. Buy the inventory items and then input the purchase in your data file.

2. Convert the Sale Order to Invoice.

3. If you used the Pending Invoice method, then mark the Invoice as final. This can be done from the Edit menu as well.

Use Pending Invoices to enter sales for which you do have inventory.

To do this:

1. Input the customer order as an Invoice.

2. Select the Edit option from the menu bar.

3. Click on Mark Invoice as Pending.

4. Buy the items and then enter them as Purchase in your file.

5. Select the Edit option from the menu bar again.

6. Click on Mark Invoice as Final.

7. Adjust the Invoice dates according to your requirement.

CHAPTER SIX

FINANCIAL STATEMENTS

Balance Sheet

A balance sheet is a document that represents the financial status or position of your enterprise at a specific point. The sheet is divided into two sections where one side shows the details of your assets, and the second side shows the equity and liabilities. The two sides should always be equal and balanced, which is why the statement is known as the balance sheet. It is easy to generate balance sheets using QuickBooks.

Let us now have a look at the various types of balance sheets.

Types of Balance Sheets

There are five types of balance sheets that can be created in QuickBooks. Let us have a look at all of them one by one.

Standard

This is a basic balance sheet. In this balance sheet, you can check out your equity, liabilities, and assets for a specific time or date.

Detail

This is the second type of balance sheet that can be generated using QuickBooks. This similar to the Standard balance sheet, but this is more detailed than the previous one. Along with the standard data, it also displays the beginning as well as ending balances of the month. It also displays the transactions that happened during the time.

Summary

This is a short report of all kinds of accounts where you can see the ending balances. It does not show the individual accounts. For instance, a general summary report will show the receivable balance of all the accounts as a total lump sum instead of showing it separately for each individual account.

Previous Year Comparison

This kind of balance sheet is useful to compare the data of the current date and the previous year's date. It can be used to trace the progress or the loss of the firm.

Class

This is another kind of balance sheet that can be created using QuickBooks. In this, the data is displayed in the form of class. This is a method employed by QuickBooks to classify your data. For instance, 'expense class' includes transportation, lodging, and food charges. For an artist, it can also include painting supplies, digital devices, assistant, postage, marketing, etc. It is necessary to assign classes to all kinds of incomes as well as expense transactions else this kind of balance sheet cannot be generated.

Generating a Balance Sheet

Generating a Balance sheet in QuickBooks is simple. To create a balance sheet:

1. Open QuickBooks.

2. Click on the File menu.

3. Click on Reports.

4. Select the Company and Financial menu.

5. Select the type of balance sheet according to your needs and requirements.

Tip

The first displayed balance sheet on the screen is always on the current date. If you want to view the balance sheet of any other date, it is necessary to enter the date in the date field. Click Refresh, and the program will generate a new balance sheet.

Income Statement

An income statement is another form of the statement that is necessary for any business. It is an important financial document. In this statement, a detailed analysis of all your business activities is mentioned. These details can be used to study and determine whether your business is making a profit or is suffering a loss.

It is essential to have this information ready all the time. It can help you to make a choice related to investing as well as spending. By studying the cash flow statement, along with the income statement and the balance statement, you can understand the total financial health of any company.

Many people who have just begun their business do not understand that there exist two kinds of income statements – the single-step version and the multi-step version. In this section, let us have a look at the difference between these two and when to use them. Understanding the difference between these two statements is important, as it will help you avoid an unnecessary hassle in the future. It can also save you a lot of time if you know what to do and how to do it.

What is an Income Statement?

In simple terms, the income statement can be defined as a detailed summary of the income of your enterprise and the expenses spent by the company over a period of time. Business owners generally analyze income statements on the basis of months, quarters, or years.

The period of income statements depends on your needs and requirements. Many people tend to use documents to track their income. For such people, it is recommended to use either monthly statements or quarterly statements. If you are planning to apply for a loan, then you need an annual income statement. QuickBooks can help you produce an income statement according to your needs instantly.

Income Statement Formats

When you generate income statements for your business, you can either use a single-step multi-step statement. These two might appear to be similar, but they are varied. Let us have a look at them one by one.

Single-Step Income Statement

Single-step income statements are easy, quick, and effortless as compared to multi-step statements. These statements can be made by deducting the total expenses from the total revenue. The result produced is net income. As it is clear that these reports only have two sections. In one part of the statement, you will find the operating as well as non-operating revenue. In the second section, you will find all the expenses, including the non-operating as well as operating expenses.

Business owners who deal with services generally use a single-step income statement because they do not have any distinct difference between the operating and non-operating contracts. Single-step income statements are easy and convenient, as they are quick and easy to make and compile.

The formula to calculate the single-step income is:

Net income or loss = total revenue - whole expenses

If the result of the above equation turns out to be positive, then you have made a net income. If the result of the above equation turns out to be negative, then you have made a net loss.

Multi-Step Income Statement

Another option to generate income statements is the multi-step income statement. This is quite similar to the single-step income statement, but it is more complex. In this form of the statement, a simple but detailed breakdown of the expenses and revenue is given in two categories. These categories are non-operating and operating.

Another aspect that makes the multi-step income statement different than the single-step income statement is that it also has a third expense category. This category is the 'Cost of Goods Sold.' This category is used to analyze and break down costs.

Operating expenses are directly related to the main activity of any business. These expenses generally include administrative expenses. Non-operating expenses are not directly related to the company and administrative expenses. These are generally related to tax expenses and interest expenses.

The people who generally produce or sell products prefer multi-step income statements. This is because, in such cases, it is crucial to keep the operating and non-operating transactions separate. The multi-step statements are generally used by retailers and manufacturers.

The formula for a multi-step income statement is:

Net income or loss = (total operating revenue + total non-operating revenue) – (total operating expenses + total non-operating expenses + cost of goods sold)

The cost of goods includes all the expenses that are necessary to produce an item. For instance, this may include the machinery, the raw materials, the manufacturing costs, etc. These costs are directly related to the production of your product. All other expenses that are related to the business but are not directly related to the production fall under the operating expenses. Administrative expenses such as wages of your employees are the required amount to run the day-to-day business smoothly.

Revenue and Expenses

An income statement is divided into two distinct categories; these are expenses and revenue. It is important to understand what these categories entail.

Revenue

Revenue is the total income that the company generates. This total income includes:

1. Operating Revenue received from the sale of services as well as goods.

2. The non-operating revenue that is gained in the form of interests acquired on loans. It also includes rent.

3. Revenue generated on sale of long-term assets such as machinery, building, vehicle, etc.

4. Other gains, including successful lawsuits.

5. The gains that are represented on income statements are different than the gross proceeds of any sale. The gains that are displayed on the income statement are the amount by which the

proceeds go beyond the asset value in the company catalogs.

If you are accustomed to the accrual accounting method and use it frequently, then you generally report your revenue on the income statement whenever you deal with goods or services. In such cases, the revenue does not depend on whether the payment has been received or not. For instance, if you perform a service, you need to consider the revenue for the income statement when you finish the work, even if you have not been paid yet. The type of payment that you will receive will be presented on the balance sheet. In such sheets, it is possible to include categories such as 'Accounts Receivable' etc., for the amount that your company owes on the balance sheet, but not on the income sheet.

It does not matter if you are paid on the spot or receive the payment sometime later in the future; the results will be the same when you calculate the revenue for the income statement. The revenues can be calculated right after the sale.

This method is useless if you decide to use the cash method of accounting, though. In the cash method of accounting, the revenue is automatically recorded when you receive the cash. For example, if you finish doing a service and give the employee the invoice after 30 days, you will able to record the revenue after a month of finishing the service.

Expenses

It is necessary to include and report all the costs that are required while producing as well as selling an item. It is also recommended to differentiate the expenses into different categories to check how you are spending the money. Some common kinds of expenses include:

1. Operating Expenses: The cost if you have overhead or payroll. Utilities, rent, insurance, publicity, communication, marketing, etc.

2. Non-Operating Expenses: This section includes all the non-core costs, such as interest expenses, an interest that is payable for debt, including loans, bonds, lines of credits, etc.

3. Costs of Goods Sold: The expenses that are directly related to the manufacturing of products. These include inventory costs, purchase of raw material, etc.

4. Losses: Losses are reported on income statements. These include losses that are incurred on lawsuit damages and the sale of assets.

Expenses also change according to the accounting method that you use. For instance, if you use the accrual method, your expenses will be reported as soon as you purchase goods or services on credit or when you receive a bill that is unfinished. In the cash method, the expense will only be recognized when you pay the bill or the invoice for the task.

Maximizing the Multi-Step Income Statement

In the last section, we saw a detailed analysis of how multi-step income statements work. In this section, let us have a look at how multi-step income statements can help you. Multi-step income statements are quite complicated as compared to the single-step statements, but they also provide you with a lot of details and data that normally cannot be accessed in the single-step income statements.

Gross Profit

One of the best things about multi-step income statements is that you can calculate the gross margin or gross profit. Calculating the gross margin is easy. Here is the formula to calculate gross profit:

Gross profit = net sales – cost of goods sold

Here is the formula to calculate the net sales:

Net sales = total sales – sales discounts – sales returns and allowances

Gross profit gives you an idea of how much money you are making after the costs of producing and selling a product are subtracted. It is an important symbol of financial stability. It is important to know how to calculate gross profit as it can help you to decide your pricing strategy. You can also use the gross profit to calculate your gross profit margin ratio. The formula to calculate the gross profit margin ratio is as follows:

Gross profit margin ratio = gross profit ÷ net sales

Gross profit margins are varied, and they change from industry to industry. It is recommended to match or exceed the gross profit margins of your enterprise. If these margins are low, it is recommended to either increase the selling price of your goods, or decrease the production costs.

Operating Income

A multi-step income statement can help you to calculate the operating income as well. The formula to calculate the operating income is as follows:

A multi-step income statement also allows you to calculate your operating income. The formula for operating income is:

Operating income = gross profit – total operating expenses

Here the gross profit allows you to understand how much money you are making from a particular service or good. The operating income allows you to understand how much profit you will gain after deducting all the business functions. For example, you notice a high-profit margin after selling a product. But after subtracting and calculating the operating income, you will see that you are not earning any profit, rather you are breaking even. This shows that your operating expenses are too much, and you need to find a method to cut these back. Operating income often includes the 'Earnings before Interest and Taxes.'

Net Income

Net income is important because it allows you to understand how much you have earned after calculating and incorporating all the expenses. In simple words, operating income decides the 'Earnings before Interest and Taxes' while the net income determines the 'Earnings after Interests and Taxes.' Here is the formula to calculate net income:

Net income = operating income + non-operating revenue – non-operating expenses – income tax expense

Once you have calculated the net income, you can use it to calculate comprehensive income as well. Comprehensive income is great as it can help you incorporate all the income that is related to business. These include the income that is generally not a part of the net income.

Business owners and firm managers can use the comprehensive income to incorporate the unrealized gains and losses. For example, the owner can incorporate the gains and losses from the firm's investments made in mutual funds or stocks. The market value of the stock needs to be higher than the amount that the owner bought it for if he or she wants to see a high comprehensive income. If the market value is lower than the purchase price, the owner will experience loss. Here is the formula to calculate comprehensive income:

Comprehensive income = net income + other comprehensive income – other comprehensive expenses

Formatting your Income Statement

Whether it is necessary to format your income statements or not solely depends on how and why you use them. For instance, if you plan to use the income statements only for internal use, then it does not matter whether you format them or not. You just need to keep the elements mentioned above accurate and correct. You can use any simple template available online to create your income statement.

In many cases, specific kinds of income statements are required. For instance, when you want to apply for a loan, banks generally ask for income statements that have been formatted in a particular and specific way. It is thus recommended to check the requirements before submitting an income statement.

This is another reason why the multi-step income statement is better than a single-step income statement. It does not matter if your expenses and revenues are straightforward; the multi-step income statement will still help you.

If you are used to a single-step income statement, you may find it difficult to use the multi-step income statement format. But, if your bank asks for it, then you will have to produce it anyhow. It is difficult to go from a single-step income statement format to a multi-step income statement format, but vice versa is simple. So it is recommended to use a multi-step income statement format whenever possible.

Compiling Income statement

As said above, income statements are absolutely critical documents for your company. It is necessary to generate at least one accurate income statement per quarter. This will help you understand the financial condition, the loss, the growth, and the value of your company. When an accurate and timely income statement is used along with a cash flow statement and a balance sheet, it can help you understand and manage the growth of your organization.

Cash Flow Statements

Cash flow can be compared to the fuel compartment of your vehicle. If you fill the compartment with fuel, it will run out slowly whenever you drive your vehicle. But if you drive too much or too quickly, you will run out of fuel. Your mission should be keeping your fuel tank full all the time. It should have at least some fuel in it all the time. Similarly, cash flow is the movement of cash in and out of your expenses. Positive cash flow is good for the company, while negative cash flow is bad for the company. It is necessary to maintain positive cash flow as much as possible.

Why is Cash Flow Important to Your Business?

For small (and many times large) business owners, positive cash flow is the ultimate goal. The owner should be able to make more money than he or she spends. While this equation sounds simple, many profitable businesses often run into cash flow issues. It is often difficult to balance the business expenses such as rent, wages, machinery, revenue, etc. with seasonal negative cash flow.

It is necessary for a small business not only to achieve a positive cash flow but to maintain it as well. In simple terms, it is necessary to check where your cash goes every month. Similarly, it is also necessary to understand how much cash you require to run the basic functions of your company.

To understand what cash flow is, it is first necessary to have a look at the cash flow statement. It is also important to learn how to read cash flow statements. This can help you to know what problems generally arise in similar businesses and how to avoid them.

What is a Cash Flow Statement?

A statement of cash flow or a cash flow statement is a statement that tracks the 'money coming in' and the 'money going out' of your enterprise. This statement records how much money your enterprise has on hand and what the liquidity of the enterprise is. It is necessary for public companies to release their cash flow statements at least every quarter.

What does a Cash Flow Statement consist Of?

Cash flow statements, income statements, and balance sheets are necessary as they help you to understand the financial condition of your company. But not many business owners know or understand how these three are connected.

The balance sheet is a record of all your finances. It is generally divided into three sections, which are liabilities, assets, and equity. The cash balance calculated using this statement is present on the balance sheet under the asset section.

The income statement is a record of the revenue, profit, loss, and expenses of an enterprise. It is good to gain insight into the financial condition of the company and whether it is gaining profit or not. The income statement is used to calculate the net income while the net income is used to calculate the cash flow. Any income that is not in the form of cash, including depreciation, affects the net income as well. These incomes go into the cash-flow statement as well.

It is thus clear that you need to have a comprehensive knowledge of all three statements if you want to understand the financial condition of your company from all angles. The cash flow statement and the balance sheet are focused on the management of the finances of your company in terms of assets and structure. The income statement is related to the central operations, which are responsible for the generation of income for your company.

Cash flow and profits are both important for your business. If you want your business to be successful and profitable in the long term, you need to have positive cash flow along with a good percentage of profit. But remember, profit does not equal cash flow as they are two distinct terms.

Cash Inflow and Outflow on your Cash Flow Statement

Businesses fail due to a variety of reasons, but one of the main reasons why they fail is because people do not understand cash flow, or they do not understand how to manage the cash flow. This is why it is necessary to understand cash inflows and outflows that are present in the cash flow statement. If you understand them and manage them properly, you will be able to keep your business running successfully.

Cash inflow is the money that goes into your company. This money comes in from a variety of sources; for instance, it can come from sales, from investments, or from financing as well. Cash outflow is the opposite of cash inflow. Cash outflow means when money goes out of your company for a variety of reasons, including disbursements, and payments to sellers, vendors, etc. If you want your company to be healthy and financially stable, your cash outflow should always be lower than the cash inflow.

You can find a variety of options on your cash flow statements. These include investing activity, operating activity, and financing activity. When the total cash gained from all these three activities is added together, you can count the overall change in cash for a particular point in time. If this amount is added to the opening cash balance, you will be able to calculate the closing cash balance.

The Difference between Cash Flow and Profit

As said above, cash flow and profit may appear to be the same thing, but they are two distinct entities in the world of accounting. To see the difference between profits and cash flow, you should compare a cash flow statement with an income statement.

The biggest difference between cash flow statements and income statements is that income statement is generally based on accrual accounting, while the cash flow statement is generally based on cash basis accounting.

Even if you do not manage your financial reporting on your own, it is still necessary to understand the basics of cash-based accounting and accrual accounting and the difference between them. This way, you can decide which form of accounting is the best for you. It is also necessary to understand that if your sales are lower than $25 million per year, you can use any of the above-mentioned methods.

Cash-Based Accounting

In the case of cash-based, revenue is mentioned when it is received, while expenses are mentioned when they are paid. This type of accounting will not recognize accounts payable and accounts receivable. Many small businesses use this method of accounting because it is quick and can be maintained with ease. It is simple to check when a transaction has been done and how much cash your business has on hand by simply checking out your bank balance quickly.

Accrual Accounting

Accrual accounting is far more complex than cash-based accounting. In this type of account, the revenues and expenses both are recorded when they are earned and not when they are paid. This means that the payment may happen immediately or after months, but the expenses and revenues will be recorded immediately.

For instance, if you pay $300 for a magazine subscription, there will be a $300 outflow from your cash flow statement. But, on the other hand, your income statement will divide the $300 into different accounting periods. These will usually be quarterly or monthly.

Imagine that you have just started a new company. After a year, you start having some cash flow issues despite your business being profitable. If you are a small business owner, you probably have invoices to collect credits and the remaining amounts from your customers. It is a well-known fact that customers rarely pay on time. Thus, even though the income statement recorded a profit for your company, you were still short on cash all the time. As you did not have cash, you could not pay your vendors on time. This is because you were not able to manage cash inflow and outflow properly — the relationship between cash flow and profit change according to the nature of your business. Sometimes you can see a lot of profit even when the cash flow is slow or inconsistent.

This means that cash flow is the money that constantly moves in or out of your business at any time. Compared to this, profit is the amount that remains after all the expenses have been deducted.

How to Read a Cash Flow Statement

Reading a cash flow statement is not a difficult job. To read it efficiently, you should break it down into the following equation:

Operating activities + financing activities+ investing activities = cash on hand

Let us now have a look at the various terms present in the above equation one by one.

Operating Activities

These activities are also known as operating cash flow. These record two things - the money you spend on a daily basis or the money you made on a daily basis. It is the money that your enterprise gains from any constant regular business activities. These activities include manufacturing, selling products, providing services, etc. This is considered to be a highly accurate assessment of how much money you gained from core business activities.

Investment Activities

These are also known as cash flow from investing activities. These assets generally include machinery, equipment, vehicles, property, investment securities, and furnishings. With time, your business becomes capable enough to pay for these investments with the help of the income created through their daily operations.

Financing Activities

Financing is the amount of cash that is either received or paid to lenders, investors, and creditors. In publicly traded companies, this section is also related to cash flow from the sale of stocks and bonds, repayment of the debt, and payment of dividends.

The cash flow equation is essential to understand the cash flow of your company.

What Causes Cash Flow Problems?

A lot of businesses have failed because the owners could not understand the difference between managing cash flow and making money. Many times, cash flow becomes a challenge because income is rarely constant, and expenses rarely sporadic. Both these affect your cash flow, but sales are never a problem related to cash flow. Sales problems are generally associated with products or sales.

There is a problem in the cash flow when the sales happen, but cash gets stuck in either account receivable or inventory. So while the sales are good, you do not have cash in hand to pay for other commodities and vendors. In simple terms, the cash is flowing in, but it is not flowing into the bank.

It is recommended to control your accounts receivable carefully as it will help you increase cash flow. There are a variety of ways through which you can get paid quickly, but many times even these methods may not work. Tracking late payments is a time-consuming task that often requires a lot of effort and money.

The best way to avoid past due receivable from growing is not to let them pile up ever. But this is not possible all the time. Some companies thus try to find some business financing options that allow them to get out of the crunch for a while. But even this can backfire sometimes.

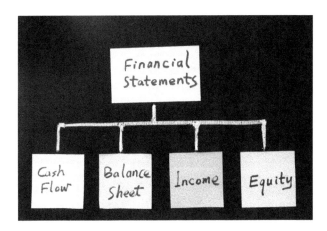

CHAPTER SEVEN

BOOKKEEPING WITH QUICKBOOKS

QuickBooks ProAdvisor

The departments of finance and accounting are always the central unit of any business. If your current properties, liabilities, and assets are confusing and are frankly a mess, and you do not know what your current financial status is, then it can lead to drastic results. It can even ruin your business forever.

A good accountant or team of accountants can make or break a business. To keep everything simple and free of chaos, it is recommended to hire a good accountant to manage your finances. The accounts are responsible for managing the financial aspects of any business. They maintain the general ledger and financial statements as well. They study the cost of operation, budgeting, and income tax returns as well.

If you are currently looking to update your business and make everything automatic and let everyone have access to the information related to business remotely, then instead of hiring a regular accountant, it is recommended to use QuickBooks ProAdvisor version. This program will help you to get a clear view of your current financial status and will also help you to understand the position in the market.

QuickBooks ProAdvisor can help you in a lot of ways. Successful businesses are rarely stagnant. They need to grow to become successful. It is necessary to hire people who can understand your business, the goals of your business, and what you are trying to achieve. Such people can then offer you proper financial advice that can help your business to grow exponentially.

Regular accountants do not have in-depth knowledge regarding QuickBooks products. This is why hiring a QuickBooks ProAdvisor is a far better option than hiring a regular accountant. A QuickBooks ProAdvisor is an experienced, well-trained, and certified professionals who can not only set up your accounts and the program but can also manage both of these things efficiently. QuickBooks ProAdvisors are experts in handling the desktop versions, as well as the online version of QuickBooks.

Every QuickBooks ProAdvisor needs to undergo strict training. They need to pass a series of tests that come after intensive training offered by Intuit. Once they pass these tests, they are certified by Intuit. The ProAdvisors need to re-take certain tests annually to update their knowledge. This keeps them up-to-date and the most trustworthy experts regarding QuickBooks.

A QuickBooks ProAdvisor can help you in a variety of ways. He or she is an expert in a lot of accounting operations, including bookkeeping. They can help you with the most complex tasks and will also help you solve the simplest of problems as well.

Here is a list of reasons that prove why it is recommended to get a QuickBooks ProAdvisor for your business if you want to achieve great success.

An Expert in QuickBooks Setup

As said above, a QuickBooks ProAdvisor is expert in everything related to QuickBooks. It is one of the most common and frequently used accounting software used by a variety of businesses all over the world. It is used to manage bills, expenses, incomes, sales, and can also study the profit levels by analyzing the complete payrolls and costs.

While using QuickBooks is quite easy, some people may find it difficult, especially in the beginning. If you do not want to be bogged down by accounting terms, it is recommended to use the proAdvisor version of QuickBooks. The ProAdvisor will do all the technical work related to QuickBooks. They can solve the problems related to accounts and can also help you understand and track cash flow and revenue as well. They can also help you if you ever run into any problem while dealing with QuickBooks.

Stay Up- To- Date on Tax Laws

QuickBooks ProAdvisors are supposed to stay updated all the time. They also tend to work hard to keep themselves updated about tax and federal changes as well as future regulations. He or she constantly study the accounting rules and regulations that are essential to keep accounting operations correct and error-free. The ProAdvisor can help you to understand the laws and can help you to tailor the objectives of your business accordingly.

ProAdvisors also try to find changes that can help you to lower inventory costs and increase revenue as well. This is essential for the growth of your business.

Provide Financial Advice and Insights

QuickBooks ProAdvisors are supposed to keep themselves updated about business development data and strategic planning options as well. They can provide you with trustworthy and essential advice that can be used to decide the best cash flow pattern, the best accounting structure, and the best financial plan that can help you to keep your business at the forefront.

They can also guess the accounting trends and other similar indicators that can help your accounting system. These are essential as they can improve the financial stability of your enterprise.

They determine accounting trends and other indicators to improve the accounting system and the company's financial position.

Businesses generally tend to grow a lot when the owners use the advice and insights provided by QuickBooks ProAdvisors. They are trained to prepare proper financial plans and can also forecast the expenses that you may have to face in the future. These things can help you to make good decisions in the future.

Training for Accounting Staff

QuickBooks ProAdvisors are experts in their field because they undergo extensive training related to QuickBooks. This makes them great coaches for other accountants as well. They can help the accounting team of any enterprise to learn the intricacies of the program. This way, the accounting team and the ProAdvisor can work efficiently together. The collaboration of the team can help you make better decisions. A well-trained team can also help you avoid mistakes and errors that can ruin a company.

The accounting team of a firm is generally led by the QuickBooks ProAdvisor. He or she coaches them and teaches them how to correct deductions, tax mistakes, and credits as well. With the help of the professional support provided by the QuickBooks ProAdvisors, the accountants can work on profits and losses, payments process, and various other accounting-related functions in an effortless, timesaving, and hassle-free manner.

Focus on Growth

One of the best things about QuickBooks ProAdvisor is that he or she can understand and explain the total costs, expenses, accounts receivables, and payables as well. They can accurately guess the taxes and can help you fill the monthly payroll tax to prevent penalties.

QuickBooks ProAdvisors can assess and identify the sections that need adjustments so that the profiles can be boosted. They work as per the accounting procedures and benchmarks. They do this to keep the fiscal health of your business intact.

QuickBooks ProAdvisors can help business owners in a variety of ways. Their help is not only restricted to planning and preparing tax. The ProAdvisors can also help the owners to expand the company, to instill good money management practices, and maintain good cash flow and tax efficiency as well. He or she does this almost without any effort.

The evaluations done by QuickBooks ProAdvisors are based on specific parameters. They can help you save time as well as money. QuickBooks ProAdvisors generate reports right out of the accounting program. They can make plans for required KPIs. They can help you keep your accounts smooth and effortless.

Along with this, the QuickBooks ProAdvisors can also guess the risks in need of mitigation. This way, the business leaders do not need to care about mitigation and can instead concentrate on their work and other aspects of the company as well.

Summary

It is necessary for every business to have a QuickBooks ProAdvisor in their team. He or she can make the complex accounting process easy, which will ensure steady growth. He or she can help you understand and interpret the financial aspects and status of your company in a better way. This will help you to understand your tax revenue, and manage your cash flow efficiently.

It is thus a great decision to seek the services of a QuickBooks ProAdvisor. This can help you to form a good business plan that can make your company a huge success.

Choosing the Right Plan

If you are a new business owner, or if you a seasoned entrepreneur, it is necessary for you to have an accounting system that will help you take your business to the next level. It is crucial that your bookkeeping software should be user-friendly. It should be able to handle all your transactions and deals. It should be up-to-date and should have all the features that are necessary in the modern world in an affordable range.

While a multitude of programs is available that can be used for accounting and bookkeeping, only a few of them can boast of possessing all the qualities mentioned above. One such brilliant accounting solution is QuickBooks. This program is great for a variety of businesses. It can help you track your inventory, can help you create reports, and can help you understand your taxes if you are self-employed, etc. Thus, QuickBooks is highly recommended for everyone who owns a business.

While QuickBooks is a versatile software, there are multiple iterations available in the QuickBooks family. It is thus quite difficult to choose the correct version that will match your needs perfectly.

QuickBooks Desktop

QuickBooks desktop has been on the market since the 1990s. It is one of the eldest and trustworthy brands in the world of accounting. A new version of QuickBooks has become highly popular in recent times. This version is called the QuickBooks Online version. It is, in a way, a stripped-down version of the desktop version. While it is true that it does not have a lot of bells and whistles like the desktop version, but it still has all the functions that are necessary for accounting and bookkeeping purposes.

In this chapter, let us have a look at different versions of QuickBooks one by one. In this particular section, we will look at QuickBooks Desktop and QuickBooks Online specifically.

QuickBooks Online

QuickBooks Online, or QBO, as it is popularly known, is a cloud-based system that has become highly popular in recent times. One of the best things about this version is that it is extremely flexible, which allows users to access the files of their company from anywhere. If your device has Internet capabilities, you will be able to access QuickBooks Online easily. You do not need to wait for your accountants or bookkeepers to send you your files as you can download them or view them from anywhere if you have a device that is capable of connecting to the Internet.

Another factor that makes QBO or QuickBooks Online really great is that it does not require any kind of installation. This means you do not need to download anything to use it. It is totally web-hosted. You just need a device connected to the Internet. All your data is collected and stored on a totally secure cloud service. Similarly, if you ever want to update your data, you can do it with ease using your web browser. This makes QuickBooks Online a safe, timesaving, effortless, and flexible option for all users.

One more feature that makes QuickBooks Online really flexible is that it allows multiple users to use the program while accessing it from multiple devices simultaneously. You do not need to pay extra for these users. There exists a user limit, though.

Within the platform, it is possible for the users to access the files of the company together. But it is recommended to avoid changing the files simultaneously as it may lead to confusion and errors. This option should be used only to view files and data.

User Limits

As said above, multiple users can use the QuickBooks Online edition simultaneously, but it has its limitations as well. All the versions of QuickBooks have different user limits. The most cost-effective version of QuickBooks Online is called Simple Start. It has all the basic features. The next subscription plan is QuickBooks Online Essential, and the most advanced and expensive subscription plan for QuickBooks Online is QuickBooks Online Plus. Each level of subscription offers different features and different user limits as well. This is why it is recommended to have a look at the features, functions, and limitations of all the editions before subscribing to any edition.

But don't worry, if you ever feel that the edition or the plan that you have subscribed is not suitable for your needs, then you can change, i.e., upgrade or downgrade the plans by contacting Intuit immediately.

Intuit decided to start the online version of QuickBooks because it realized that a lot of professionals were demanding such a version. As the world is changing rapidly, people want to stay connected all the time. They want to stay connected with their data, and they believe that they should be able to access it anytime, anywhere. This desire is also closely related to the desire of having a SAAS or software as a service. People who want a SAAS believe that paying to upgrade software applications on a system does not make any sense. It is thus no wonder that this version has become so popular among customers, users, and professionals all around the world. It has become a boon for small business owners who are generally on the road for a long time. It is true that it is slightly expensive as compared to the purchase of the desktop version, but it is surely worth it. If the features of QuickBooks Online is compared with other QuickBooks products, it is clear that it has all the features and more of QuickBooks Pro 2011. This makes it highly suitable for users who indulge in various vocations and businesses.

One of the best things about using the online version of QuickBooks is that you do not need to worry about your data. Your data is stored online on the cloud, which means that it will stay safe no matter what. It will never crash. It is continuously backed up and can be accessed from anywhere and at any time. You just need a device with an Internet connection to access your data. This flexibility and ease of use have made QuickBooks Online a highly popular program.

Versions

Currently, there are five different versions of QuickBooks Online that are available on the market. Out of these five, we have already seen the first three versions briefly. The following are the five versions of QuickBooks Online:

1. Online Simple Start

2. Online Essentials

3. Online Plus

4. Online Essentials with Payroll

5. Online Plus with Payroll

Let us now have a look at all these versions one by one.

Simple Start

As said above, the Simple Start version is the least expensive version of QuickBooks Online. It is the most basic version of QuickBooks, and it does not have a lot of features. It is generally considered to be of no use for many businesses. You cannot import the

QuickBooks Desktop version files into it. Similarly, it does not allow you to make invoices, conduct online banking, does not allow you to make bills, does not allow you to use a purchase order, it has no option to take company snapshots, and it does not allow you to track time either. These options are quite affordable, but as it does not offer a lot of features, many people generally tend to go for upgrades immediately. This is a good starting point to learn the basics, but it is recommended to use a more advanced version.

Online Essentials

This is the 'standard' version of the accounting service. It can be used to run a simple normal business. It is true that you cannot create a bill by the customer, but it is still a highly suitable version. Other features that are not available in this version include multiple location tracking, purchase order, class tracking, inventory tracking, planning, and budgeting. These features are available in the Online Plus version of QuickBooks Online. If you have a product-based service, it is recommended to go for Online Plus instead of using the Essentials. This will help you to keep things simple.

Many accountants and experts agree with the above point. If you have simple accounting needs, then subscribing to QuickBooks Online is the best option for you. If you believe that you require a lot of complex accounting needs, then it is recommended to go for the desktop version of the program instead. The desktop version is well suited to handle the heavy load.

Tip

If you ever decide to cancel your subscription of QuickBooks Online, the software will still keep your data for a month. You can export this data to either a spreadsheet or to the Desktop version of the program. This data cannot be changed or edited on the cloud. If you do not download the data before a year, the data will disappear, and you will not be able to access it afterward.

QuickBooks Desktop vs. QuickBooks Online

The online version of QuickBooks is great for all small-scale businesses. This version is also good for consultants as well as freelancers. These people generally need a service that is simple and flexible. QuickBooks Online provides them these functions.

As mentioned above, many different users can use and access the cloud-based software together in real-time. Another great thing about this version is that the data is backed up and synced automatically to the cloud.

These are some of the features that are available in QuickBooks Online but are not available in QuickBooks Desktop.

- You can upload and backup documents, files, and images from a mobile device or tablet.

- You can send and schedule automatic transactions.

- You can auto register banks.

- You can download the bank transactions automatically at night.

- The option of custom splitting, which is based on percentage or amount.

- You can also assign location rules and classes.

- You can audit logs and review the actions.

- You can track changes as well.

- You can give seven different names to the customer.

- You can delay credits and charges for any non-posting transactions that will be billed later.

- Multi-line journal entries are available for Accounts Receivable and Account Payable.

- Multi-fiscal year budgeting capabilities.

- It can be integrated seamlessly with many different third-party apps such as Bill.com, Tsheets, and Expensify.

- Free 30-day trial period

QuickBooks Desktop

QuickBooks Desktop has a multitude of benefits and solutions that make it one of the best accounting and bookkeeping apps for any business. There are some problems associated with QuickBooks Desktop; for instance, you need to buy a user license for each and every individual user. So, unlike QuickBooks Online, multiple users cannot use it simultaneously unless you are ready to pay this extra amount. Each separate user and each separate computer will have to pay a separate license fee as well. This is why some people do not use QuickBooks Desktop.

There are three different versions of QuickBooks Desktop available on the market; they are called the QuickBooks Pro, QuickBooks Premier, and QuickBooks Enterprise. Some features and tools are available in only Enterprise and Premier versions and are not available in the Pro version. A detailed analysis of these three versions is available in the next section.

QuickBooks Online vs. QuickBooks Desktop

The Desktop version of QuickBooks is extremely robust and full of features. It has a lot of product-based as well as accounting features. This is why companies that are focused on products generally use the Desktop version to manage their accounts. This is especially true in the case of small businesses. This system is great for financial tracking and inventory tracking, as well. These two are important as they allow users to understand the profitability of sales and expenses. They can also help you to forecast things that generally require users to purchase third party applications and add-ons.

Features

Here is a list of major features that are only available in the QuickBooks Desktop version but are not available in QuickBooks Online version.

The following features are available via QuickBooks Desktop but are not supported via QBO.

Reporting Capabilities

1. It offers industry-specific reporting

2. It offers impeccable business planning and forecasting

3. You can create balance sheet by class options as well

4. It offers multiple customization offers for footer and header

Another great feature that the Desktop version offers is Scheduled Reporting. This feature was added to the program in 2017. It enables users to create scheduled reports. This can help the user to create scheduled reports which can be sent using email directly. This is brilliant for the finances of the company. It also helps you to save a lot of time and effort in the long term.

Accounting Benefits

- It can print the Form 1099-MISC

- It can create the Produce Period Copy

- It offers a variety of client data review options and tools

- It offers backup and restore options for accountants

- It can clean files

- It can correct unapplied payments and credits

- It can send you reminders to deposit undeposited funds

- It can fix sales tax errors

Data Entry

- It can generate Invoice Batches

- It can create batch transactions

- It can customize billing rate levels

- The payroll can take in batched timesheets as well

Inventory Features

The Desktop version of QuickBooks has many different inventory features; they include:

- Sales Order Tracking

- Unit of Measurement Inventory

- Valuation Method for Average Cost of Inventory

- Purchase Order Process Receiving Capabilities

- Custom Inventory Reorder Scheduling

A lot of custom features have been added to QuickBooks Desktop that is similar to the features of QuickBooks Online. The main motive behind this is to make the Desktop version as user-friendly as possible. This way, it becomes highly suitable for all users who do not want to handle a difficult to use software but do not want to forgo on the robustness of the program either.

How to Choose?

The choice between QuickBooks Desktop and QuickBooks Online is a difficult one. There are many pros and cons of both the products that should be considered before buying any version. Here is a small list of aspects and areas that you can consider before making a choice for your business. Let us have a look at them one by one:

Customization

QuickBooks Desktop has a lot of customization options. For instance, you can customize expense categories, forms, and can also track employee mileage as well. These customization options are not available in QuickBooks Online.

Cost

QuickBooks Online is great because it has a 30-day trial period, but after 30 days, the user needs to pay a subscription fee, which is usually monthly. Compared to this, you need to pay only a one-time fee to use the desktop version. The cost of the product solely depends on the product that you have selected. It can either be Pro, Premier, or Enterprise.

Automated Functions

QuickBooks Online is a great option for people who only deal with things such as downloading bank transactions, customer billing, and payment processing. Most of these things are generally done manually using QuickBooks Desktop. Nowadays, thanks to the new update, QuickBooks Desktop now offers automatic reporting as well.

Accessibility

QuickBooks Online can be accessed from any device in the world that is connected with the Internet. Compared to this, QuickBooks Desktop can only be accessed using the device on which it has been installed. The device needs to have the license for this access as well. QuickBooks Online is based on the cloud; this means that it can be accessed remotely as well.

QuickBooks Desktop to QuickBooks Online

Intuit is enabling more and more people to use QuickBooks Online. This is because the business keeps on evolving, and a lot of business now happens on the cloud. People who generally use QuickBooks Desktop can shift to QuickBooks Online using the following option:

1. Open QuickBooks Desktop

2. Click on Company.

3. Click on Export Company File to QuickBooks Online

4. Click on Help

5. Click on Update QuickBooks

6. Click on All updates from the Update Now Window

7. Click on Get Updates

8. Click on Close

9. Click on File Menu

10. Click Exit.

11. Restart QuickBooks and let the installation process finish. This process usually takes around 15 minutes to finish, but it may take even longer if you haven't updated for a long time.

12. Enter your login details for QuickBooks Online.

13. Click on Agree to Terms of Service.

14. Click Submit.

15. Choose the online company you want to import the data into. You can also generate a new company.

16. Click OK.

17. You will soon receive an email from QuickBooks.

Which Version is best for you?

As it is clear from above that the QuickBooks Desktop version and the QuickBooks Online version are quite different and have their own sets of pros and cons. The decision solely depends on which version to get.

Once again, the QuickBooks Desktop version is designed for people who want to use customized budgeting and reporting options. Similarly, it is also great for users who do not want to pay a monthly subscription charge. The users who prefer desktop versions usually do not care about online access and remote access to the books. They do not care if they cannot access their books all the time.

It should be noted that all the businesses do not need all the functions and features that QuickBooks Desktop has to offer. This is okay. If you do not know which version to choose, it is recommended to try out the 30-Day Trial for QuickBooks Online version. You can also use other applications to fill in the gaps that the QuickBooks Online version has. It should be noted that most of the third-party apps will charge you some money. They generally have an annual or a monthly subscription amount.

QuickBooks Desktop Versions and Others

As said above, there are multiple versions of QuickBooks Desktop. In this section, let us have a look at these versions in detail. Along with these versions, this section will also cover some other versions of QuickBooks.

In the beginning, Intuit, the parent company of QuickBooks, offered only one version of QuickBooks. But with time, the technology has evolved, and now Intuit has created a variety of versions of the program.

QUICKBOOKS

These various options include QuickBooks Mac, QuickBooks Online, QuickBooks Simple Start, QuickBooks Standard, QuickBooks Pro, QuickBooks Enterprise, and QuickBooks Premier. There are also other varieties, such as industry-specific versions of QuickBooks. These versions are often customized according to the enterprise or industry. If you do not want to use a specific industrial version of QuickBooks, you can also use a regular version of QuickBooks and customize it according to your needs and requirements.

Due to a multitude of options that are available, users may find it quite daunting to select a version of QuickBooks that will fulfill their needs. This section will help you learn how to choose between different versions of QuickBooks.

As said above, choosing between different versions of QuickBooks is difficult. Many people think that the more money you pay, the better suited the program will be. Many times, the most expensive programs have a lot of functions and features. But if you do not need such features, it is recommended to avoid such a version. There are only two things that you need to consider when buying QuickBooks. These two things are your needs and requirements. For instance, if you do a lot of daily transactions and financial deals as well, you will need a good accountant. If such a person decides to use the simplest and least expensive version of QuickBooks, his or her business will suffer a lot. Similarly, a person has just started a business and is looking to expand it by using accounting software and decided to get the most expensive. This person, too, will suffer the fate of a misguided choice. Both these people will not only waste a lot of money and effort, but they will also lose a lot of important time as well. It is thus recommended to make choices correctly.

But then how do you make a choice when there are so many options available on the market? Is it worth paying the extra amount to buy Premier? Is QuickBooks Online sufficient for my business, or should I get something else? These and many other questions are quite popular related to QuickBooks. If you, too, are plagued by the question of choice, this section will help you make the correct decision regarding which version of QuickBooks to buy.

There are many different versions of QuickBooks, and each industry or enterprise needs a different version. But almost all businesses can make do with QuickBooks Pro, as it is a good combination of features, ease of use, and affordable. But it is still recommended to think wisely before choosing this version. QuickBooks is not cheap software, and many versions of the program retail for several hundred dollars. If you buy a QuickBooks version without checking whether it suits your company or not, you will lose a lot of money.

This section will try to cover all the different varieties of QuickBooks in brief. This brief information regarding the QuickBooks versions will help make your choice quickly and effortlessly. It will also provide you multiple options according to your needs or requirements.

QuickBooks Versions

Let us now have a look at the different versions of QuickBooks that are currently available on the market.

QuickBooks for Mac

This has been placed here because this is the easiest decision to make. If your company uses predominantly (or perhaps) only Mac operating system, then you need to use QuickBooks Mac. There are currently no other QuickBooks options available from Intuit that can be used on Macs (except the Online version, which can be used on any device with an Internet connection). QuickBooks Mac is quite different from any other desktop version of QuickBooks because it is, in a way, a software package that contains a multitude of different products that are not available in other Desktop packages offered by QuickBooks. Barring the QuickBooks Online and QuickBooks Mac, all other versions of QuickBooks run on Windows. QuickBooks Mac has been specially devised and created in such a way that it can integrate and work properly with the Mac interface and framework. You can use the different functions, modules, features, and sections of this software without forgoing the Mac features. In the beginning, QuickBooks Mac was complicated and difficult to use. It was not user-friendly at all. But with time, Intuit has developed far better products. Now the Mac version of QuickBooks looks like a proper Mac application and works like one as well. The new editions of QuickBooks Mac can be integrated with various other services, including iCal for calendar-related features and MobileMe for backups and restoration processes.

Another positive factor with QuickBooks is that it is possible to share data from QuickBooks Desktop (Windows) to QuickBooks Mac and vice versa. This is a great option when your accountant uses QuickBooks Mac, and you use QuickBooks Windows.

While Intuit does not have a Premier version for QuickBooks Mac, the regular version will suffice the needs of common users. But if you need extremely advanced capabilities and functionalities, then you need to get a Windows PC and use the Windows version of QuickBooks. If you do not want to get a Windows PC, you can also try a Windows Emulator to use the Windows program.

QuickBooks Pro

QuickBooks Pro is perhaps the most downloaded and highly popular version of QuickBooks. This is because it is affordable, it is cost-effective, and it contains almost all the commonly required functions and tools that are necessary for day-to-day accounting. If you really want to take your business to the next level, then QuickBooks Pro can help you a lot. If you want more capabilities, then it is recommended to go QuickBooks Premier instead.

QuickBooks Pro has a variety of features that are explained below:

- It can help you track your expenses.

- It can help you track your bills.

- It can help you print checks.

- It can help you track sales.

- It can help you create new and track customer accounts.

- It has good payroll management capabilities.

- It can generate invoices and reports.

- It can create estimates.

- Using a service, it can accept credit cards as well.

- You can do batch invoicing using this QuickBooks version.

- Three users can use the program simultaneously.

- You can track expenses as well as time for specific clients with ease.

QuickBooks Premier

QuickBooks Premier is a highly advanced version of QuickBooks. It is more focused on vertical industries and enterprises. Usually, contractors, general business owners, manufacturers, wholesale sellers, people who offer professional services, and people in retail use QuickBooks Premier. This version of QuickBooks is highly customizable, and you can change a lot of details in it. For instance, even the name of the objects changes according to the industry. Thus, Customers become Donors if you use this version for a non-profit organization. This makes QuickBooks Premier a versatile and flexible application.

Along with the features present in QuickBooks Pro, the QuickBooks Premier has some more features. These include:

- It can help you create a business plan

- It can help you forecast expenses and sales

- It can help you track balance sheet by class

- It has an option of industry-specific reporting

QuickBooks Enterprise

QuickBooks Enterprise is Intuit's foray into the large, industrial level business world. The Enterprise version of QuickBooks has the option to have more data sets. These data sets fall under the range of 14,500 limits to 1,000,000 limits. This is absolutely necessary for large businesses. Generally, large businesses have a large number of accountants as well. This range can help the accountants do their jobs with ease.

The Enterprise version of QuickBooks is great for companies where more users need to use the program. It also offers other functionalities such as more audit trails and good integration capabilities. You can integrate the program with various other business systems.

This version is surely expensive, but if you really have a huge industry, then it is recommended to get this version.

This is the best accounting software for you if you have a large organization. Using other versions of QuickBooks will only waste your time, as they will not be able to handle your operations properly. Thus, instead of wasting time, money, and effort on other accounting software, it is recommended to get QuickBooks Enterprise immediately.

How to Decide Which QuickBooks to Buy

Until now, we have covered the variety of versions of QuickBooks that are available on the market. In the last section, we saw how to choose between QuickBooks Online and QuickBooks Desktop. If you have decided to go with QuickBooks Desktop, this section will help you choose between the three versions of the program. All the different versions of QuickBooks software have their own pros and cons. It is thus your duty to make a list of your requirements and the needs of your firm before making a decision. You should also check out all the features of the programs once again and then finally select a version of QuickBooks that will suit your requirements. Avoid getting something too basic or equally something too advanced. This section will help you narrow down your choices significantly.

If you are a Mac user, then the best option for you is obviously QuickBooks Mac. But it is not your only choice. You can also use QuickBooks Online. If you want to use QuickBooks Premier or QuickBooks Pro on a Mac, it is possible. You just need to install a Windows Emulator on your Mac. But it is recommended to use a dedicated Windows PC instead.

If you need a lot of remote access and want to access your data any time anywhere, then QuickBooks Online is the best option for you. This is a great option for organizations that are quick-paced and contemporary. This version is really popular with people who like to have access to their data all the time.

Nowadays, some other versions of QuickBooks have started offering the anytime, anywhere data option as well. For instance, QuickBooks Pro now offers a service through which you can switch on mobile and remote data access. You just need to pay a small monthly service fee to use this feature. But the overall price to use this feature is high, but if you need anywhere, anytime access, this is appealing to many people. This is because you need to pay the regular licensing fee along with the monthly subscription charges to use this feature. If you really want to access your data remotely in an affordable manner, then QuickBooks Online is the best program for you.

If you want a program that can be industry-specific, then QuickBooks Premier is the best option for you. It has a lot of features and tools that are well suited for various industries. They offer a lot of control options. This is why QuickBooks Premier is the best option for industries.

If you buy a lot of raw materials and manufacturing materials and want to keep and track inventory for the options, then QuickBooks Pro is the best option for you. If you think that this version is not able to handle your inventory properly, then it is recommended to go for a more advanced version of QuickBooks, such as the QuickBooks Premier.

If you have a small business and you do not need a lot of accounting features, then QuickBooks Pro is a good option for you. It can handle all the needs and requirements of a small firm. It is a great asset to accountants. If you want to use a small business program package, the QuickBooks Pro will really help you.

As said above, there are many different versions of QuickBooks with a variety of pros and cons. Just check what your business needs and choose the appropriate version accordingly.

Becoming a Certified QuickBooks ProAdvisor

There are many different bookkeeping programs available on the market. QuickBooks is one such program that is generally used by small businesses as well as other individuals as well.

Intuit, the parent company of QuickBooks, has a variety of programs to help you and fulfill all your accountancy and bookkeeping needs. One such program is QuickBooks ProAdvisor. This version allows you to hire accountants to help you. Similarly, you can get certified from Intuit using this version. The company generally certifies people who are proficient in using QuickBooks. They just need to take an exam to get this.

There are other certificates available from various firms such as NACPB or the National Association of Certified Public Bookkeepers that prove that you are proficient in QuickBooks.

Part 1

Preparing for the Certification Exam

Step One:

Before beginning the certification process, it is necessary to ask yourself why you need the certification. Many individuals can find the certificate unnecessary. It is true that you cannot claim that you have been certified by QuickBooks unless you take the exam and receive the certificate, but it does not mean that you cannot become proficient in the program without the certificate. You can master the software without the certificate with the help of training and self-learning. Another aspect of the certificate is that it is only related to QuickBooks. This means that the certificate does not help you with other accounting software that is available on the market. If your employers or clients think that you should be able to use other software along with QuickBooks, then this certificate will not help you in a significant way.

QuickBooks is just one of the many accounting programs available on the market. But what makes it one of the best ones is that it incorporates a lot of different accounting functions and options. But this does not mean that a QuickBooks certification can make you an accredited accountant. The certificate cannot make you a certified accountant or bookkeeper.

Step Two:

Intuit believes that it is necessary for people to have at least two years' experience before using QuickBooks for functions related to invoicing and payroll. Intuit also recommends having a two-year experience for creating cost reports and budgeting as well. But there exist no formal requirements or eligibility issues for the process of certification. A user can take the certification exam whenever he or she believes that he or she has the necessary skills and needs.

It should be noted that QuickBooks certificate is not necessary for business owners, bookkeepers, and people who are already experts in using the software. The certificate is necessary if you want to use the official logo and certification on your business accounts and resume. It thus serves as a marketing tool that can help you attract a lot of employees and customers as well. Nowadays, many employers seek people with QuickBooks expertise, so having a QuickBooks certificate can help you stand out from the crowd.

Step Three:

It is recommended to understand what is expected in the exam and what you should expect from the exam. Generally, the following skills will be put to the test in the exam:

- How to set up the software

- How to work with lists

- Using various bank accounts

- Input data in invoices and sales

- Using other QuickBooks accounts

- Entering as well as paying bills

- Receiving payments

- Making deposits

- Analyzing financial data

Step Four:

It is recommended to check out the variety of certificates that are available and choose one that perfectly fits with your needs and requirements. Intuit has different levels of training and certification. The certification is supposed to be a marketing tool that can be used to get better offers from employers and customers. So it is recommended to get a certificate that can help you target your 'target demographic.' Do not apply for random certificates if you believe that they will not help you. Instead, it is recommended to contact an expert and ask for his or her advice while choosing a certificate level. This will help you keep your journey towards certification effortless. Here is a list of various certification levels that are currently available:

ProAdvisor without Certification:

In this level, you get QuickBooks training material, but you do not receive any certificate. You will be able to learn all the basics of QuickBooks and understand some intricacies as well.

1. ProAdvisor with Certification in QuickBooks Pro/Premier: For this level, you need to take a simple test that will test you on many different functions of QuickBooks Premier and Pro. Passing this test will get you a certificate.

2. ProAdvisor with Certification in Intuit QuickBooks Enterprise Solutions: this level also involves a certification test, but this test is more complex than the one above. It is more focused on the QuickBooks Enterprise version.

3. ProAdvisor with Certification in QuickBooks Point of Sale: It is a complex test. This test and training are focused on the QuickBooks Point of Sale products.

4. Advanced Certified ProAdvisor: This is the most difficult test of all the tests. You need to take a complex test to get the certificate. In this test, you will also be tested for advanced functions of the program, troubleshooting

problems, errors, using third party applications, job costing, and many other areas as well.

Step Five:

As said above, it is necessary to decide whether a training course and certificate are correct for you or not. If you are not confident about your current knowledge regarding QuickBooks, then it is recommended to join a QuickBooks training class. Here you can learn how to use QuickBooks efficiently, after which you can take the certification exam that you want and need. There are a variety of classes available now. Some of them are online, while a lot of them are offline as well. Some options include:

Official in-person or offline training is given by Intuit Academy. Many people think that taking a class devised by Intuit will help them become better than any other class, but this is just a myth. You can take classes anywhere; it does not matter.

1. An Authorized accounting firm: There are many different, authorized firms that offer various training courses. They also offer certificate courses.

2. Bookkeeping class: It is also possible to classes on QuickBooks from various Bookkeeping institutes and classes. This is great if you want

to learn QuickBooks but do not care about certification, as this method allows you to learn everything without taking the certification exam. It is necessary to check whether the class or institute is accredited or not. If the class is not accredited, avoid it.

Step Six:

Study Guides:

Another factor that can help you with the certification exam is getting a study guide. Nowadays, a lot of study guides are available on the market according to the level of difficulty. It should be noted that the certification exam is an open-book test. This is why getting a study guide is absolutely crucial as you can use it in the exam for references as well.

There are many different study guides available for QuickBooks. Many different websites offer free online tutorials, as well. These free tutorials can help you understand the difficult parts of the program.

There are also many paid versions of tutorials and study guides available on the market. Choose wisely.

Part 2

Taking the Certification Exam

Step One:

It is recommended to take as many practice exams as possible before taking the real exam. There are many practice exams available online that can help you to be prepared. You can find many practice tests by Intuit as well as other services as well. They are not necessary for the certification, but they can really help you to be well prepared. It is recommended to take at least two practice exams. The time for these practice exams is two hours, just like the official exam. As the official exam is an open book test, it is recommended to use your study guide while taking the practice exams as well.

Step Two:

To take the exam for QuickBooks certification, you need to sign up for it. The exam is overseen by the National Association of Certified Public Bookkeepers (NACPB). You are supposed to take the exam online with the ATTC or the Accountant Training and Testing Center.

Once you are ready to take the certification exam, just visit the ATTC website and click on the Schedule a Test page. Here you can choose the time and date on which you want to take the test. The ATTC will send you all the relevant details related to your exam on email.

It should be noted that while the test is offered by the official bookkeeping association, it is still related to QuickBooks only. It does not mean that you are a certified bookkeeper or an accountant. It only proves that you are proficient at QuickBooks.

The fee for the test is $150 if you are not a member of NACPB, but if you are a member of the NACPB, then you are supposed to pay $100 for the same.

If you fail the exam, you can retake the exam by paying a smaller fee. This fee is $50 for members of NACPB and $75 for nonmembers of NACPB.

Step Three:

The third step is obviously taking the exam itself. The exam has a fairly easy format. There are 50 MCQs or multiple-choice questions and simulations. To clear the exam successfully, you need to score at least 75%. This means that you need to solve at least 37 questions correctly. But don't worry, the exam is two hours long and is an open-book test. This means that you can consult with your book and check it while writing the test. Once you successfully clear the exam, you will receive an official certificate from the organization. You will also receive the certification logo, which you can use on your cards, banners, etc. This will help you attract potential employers as well as clients who want people proficient in QuickBooks.

As said above, even if you fail the exam, you can retake it for a discounted fee. It is recommended to stay up-to-date and keep your certificate up-to-date as well. You need to retake certain tests from time to time to keep your certificate up-to-date. This is necessary because QuickBooks changes a lot as the company keeps on introducing new features and functions. It is thus recommended to update your training and certificate every year. This will help you stay updated, relevant, and popular among employers. It will also help you attract a lot of clients who want an accountant who keeps himself or herself updated all the time.

CHAPTER EIGHT

QUICKBOOKS TIPS

Until now, we have seen the basics and important aspects of QuickBooks and how it can change your life. QuickBooks is surely one of the best business and bookkeeper software packages available on the market. It is well known for its variety of security features along with an elegant, sophisticated, and easy to use interface. It has a variety of features that make it the best software for accounting. It has multiple features, such as employee management, bank integration, etc. that make it highly popular and usable. While the learning curve of QuickBooks is not as steep as other software, beginners may still find it a bit difficult. It has many shortcuts and tips that can make your overall experience with the software easy. Even if you are an experienced user, it is possible that you may not know about all the secrets and tips that the software is hiding. This chapter will cover many different, useful, and crucial tips that will help you use QuickBooks in a far more efficient manner. Let us have a look at these tips one by one. These tips will surely help you become a master of QuickBooks.

Use ProAdvisor

This is a highly recommended tip for people who have just started using QuickBooks. ProAdvisor is a part of the Intuit Package. It is extremely useful as it allows you to connect with a local accountant. The accountant can help you with the software and other aspects as well. For instance, the accountant can also give you crucial advice on topics such as tax requirements and business structure. He or she can also teach you how to offset expenses. Thus, this option can help you prevent frustration and can help you save a lot of time as well.

Take Your Time to Understand the Basics

As said earlier, QuickBooks has learned, though not as steeply as other software. But this does not mean that an inexperienced or new user will find himself or herself at home right from the first use. You will surely need to spend some time to understand the basics of the software. One of the best ways to learn the basics of the software is by using the 'Getting Started Tutorials' options. In this option, you will learn how to manage bills, how to input costs, and various other aspects as well.

All the tutorials under the above option are extremely well made and well constructed. They are highly practical, as well. To avoid frustration later, it is recommended to invest a few hours on the tutorials in the beginning. These tutorials are sure to help you understand the basics of the software.

Passwords are Essential

Like your money, your financial data is crucial as well. Data theft has become a serious issue now. If you do not use a strong password, your hard-earned money may get stolen. It is necessary to choose a strong and difficult to guess the password to avoid any problems in the future. People generally connect their QuickBooks account with their bank accounts. If your QuickBooks gets hacked due to a weak password, the hacker will be able to access your bank details and accounts as well. Thus, to avoid any future problems, risks, and frustrations, it is recommended to choose a strong password. Never share your password, and do not write it down. Do not use passwords that can be guessed with ease. These include birthdays, anniversaries, phone numbers, etc.

If you cannot come up with a complex password, you can also use an online password creator.

Enter Correct Company Information

When you put the details regarding your firm into the software, do it correctly. Everything that you add to the software should be accurate. This includes your reporting forms, business structure, calendars, Tax ID number, etc. If you input the wrong data into the system, it may lead to serious problems later. It is recommended to enter all the correct details regarding your firm using the 'Company Tab.' It is always better to crosscheck the data before submitting it.

Input Accurate Customer Details

Like Company or Firm details, you should always enter the correct Customer details in your system. It is necessary to learn and understand the basics of how to set up a new customer in the system. To do this, just click on the Customers tab at the center of the screen and then input all the details. It is necessary to add to each customer as a new customer. It is also recommended to customize their payment options as a check, cash, or credit card.

If you are new to the world of QuickBooks, it is recommended to set up your core customers as soon as possible and then add new customers whenever they come. The user needs to be disciplined about this as it will help him or her to avoid further inconveniences. It will also make other tasks such as reconciliation and invoicing easy.

Inputting Employee Details

Many people use QuickBooks to pay their employees; if you are one of them, then it is recommended to understand the Employee related options carefully. QuickBooks can help you manage deductions, tax payments, benefits, etc. To utilize these features, just go to the Employees Tab. In this tab, you will find the Employees Center. Here you can set up employees in a quick and efficient manner. You can also view the reports in this section.

Reconciling on QuickBooks

While QuickBooks is already a great, efficient, and quick way to manage your books, you can make it even better with the help of constant reconciliation. It is necessary to reconcile your accounts regularly. This way, you will always have an idea of what is going on in your business. It is especially recommended to reconcile your accounts when you receive a statement or remittance. You should reconcile whenever you receive statements for loans, credit cards, bank accounts, etc.

Backing up QuickBooks

It is recommended to back up your data from time to time to keep it safe and secure. The best way to ensure that your data is being backed up or not is by setting an automatic schedule. Backing up your data needs to be one of your most important priorities. If you do not back up your QuickBooks (and if it is present on only one system), and the system crashes, you will lose your complete data.

Integrate your QuickBooks with your backup software to avoid data loss. You can also use the online version of QuickBooks. These versions back up your data directly to the Cloud. This way, you will never lose your data.

Print Checks Directly from QuickBooks

Printing check frequently is a highly time-consuming and expensive task. If you want to save a lot of time and money, you can print your checks using QuickBooks. Printing checks is easy; just click on the Banking Tab and click Write Check. Here click on Print. You will not have paycheck fees to your bank anymore.

Paying Bills via QuickBooks

Paying bills using QuickBooks is easy and timesaving. You can do this by using the Online Bill Payment Option. Using this method, you can avoid all unnecessary steps, and you can reconcile your accounts in no time. This will save you a lot of effort and time in the long term.

Customize Your QuickBooks' Layout

QuickBooks is extremely user-friendly. It allows users to change the interface and customize it according to their needs and desires. If you are accustomed to the old interface, you can change it back so easily. Just click on Edit, followed by Preferences, followed by Desktop View. Here you can change and customize the desktop according to your desire.

Customize Your Icon Bar

It is also possible to customize the Icon Bar in QuickBooks. Icon Bar is a timesaving option present in QuickBooks. Here you can put the link that you require and use the most. To customize your Icon bar, click on View, followed by Customize Icon Bar. Now customize the bar according to your usage.

Utilize Memorized Transactions

You can use QuickBooks to make your life simple. It allows you to make regular transactions automatically. To use this feature, just click on Lists, followed by Memorized Transaction List, followed by Memorized Transaction, followed by New Group. Here you can set up all the transactions that you want to be remembered. These can be used to send patterned monthly invoices or pay patterned bills.

Use Online Banking

QuickBooks can help you do online banking with ease. QuickBooks integrates online banking and makes it simple. To use Online Banking in QuickBooks, just click on the Online Banking option on the Icon Bar. A tutorial will begin. Once you finish the tutorial, you can start using online banking immediately. Be careful, though! It is recommended to pay close attention to your security. If more than one user utilizes the software, then it may lead to catastrophic results.

Setting Up 1099 Vendors

Many people use freelancers and contractors for help. Managing and keeping track of their transactions is a difficult problem that can be solved with ease using QuickBooks. It is possible to set up 1099 Vendors using QuickBooks. Using this option, you can sort your payments along with sales taxes to the independent freelancers. This will help you save a lot of time and frustration at the end of the year.

Turning Off Spellcheck

Spellcheck may seem to be a strange feature in QuickBooks, but many people find it useful and crucial. But if you are one of those people who do not like using this, you can shut it off. To turn spellcheck off, just click on Edit. Next, click on Preferences, followed by Speller. Click on the box next to Always Check Spelling to turn the feature off.

Restricting User Access

If you believe that your software is being used by a lot of people and you think that it is a problem, then you can restrict user access as well. It is advisable to restrict user access because QuickBooks deals with a lot of intricate and sensitive data and functions. To restrict user access, the best way is to create multiple users and give them access to specific features only. This way, users can use the accounts for specific tasks only, and your personal data will remain safe.

Online Payments via QuickBooks

Another great feature of QuickBooks is that you can accept payments from the customers directly while simultaneously reducing the fees as well. To do this, you just need to enter and set up your bank details. These details can then be used by the customers to pay you directly. Each transaction only costs around 50 cents, which makes it a lucrative and highly affordable option. It is cheaper than many other options that are available on the market. Instead of considering these options and wasting your time, it is recommended to use QuickBooks simply.

Find the History of a Transaction

Finding invoices, memos, credit memos, payments, related invoices, and sorting them can be a time-consuming and difficult task. Managing these receipts and sorting them and storing them according to the records can take a lot of time. QuickBooks can help you save a lot of time by providing you a simple and elegant way to find the history of any transaction. Just click on the Reports option and then click on Transaction History. The history of all your transactions and related data will be displayed instantaneously.

Linking Your Email to QuickBooks

Nowadays, many people offer online services or have businesses that do not need any kind of physical invoices. In such businesses, it may become difficult to keep track of transactions. To solve this problem, just link your email account to QuickBooks. This way, you can send your invoices directly to the customer. You can also enable the option to receive email reports. You can link a variety of emails to your QuickBooks, including Gmail, Outlook, Yahoo, etc.

Viewing Double Entries

QuickBooks, like all other accounting systems, uses the Double Entry principle. This ensures its smooth functionality and adaptability. To check the double-entry of any transaction, just open the transaction and go to the Reports>Transaction Journal. This will help you to open a Transaction Journal. In this journal, you can check whether the double-entry has been posted properly or not.

Merging Similar Accounts

Sometimes, due to multiple accounts, a QuickBooks file may become too complex and heavy. This generally happens when different accounts are created by different employees for different tasks. This also happens when multiple customer accounts are created due to manual errors.

To make the process easy and manage the accounts efficiently, you can use the merging option. To merge, simply choose an account name and select the second account to merge it with. Right-click and paste the name of the account that you want to merge. Once done, click on save. This will successfully merge the accounts.

Chat with Staff

In QuickBooks, the staff has an option to use different accounts to chat using the QuickBooks window. Using this, your team can discuss entries and solve problems simultaneously. Using the chat option is easy. Just open the Company menu and click the Chat with a Coworker option. This will initiate a new chat.

Offset Invoices against Credit Notes

If you offset zero against credit notes, a lot of invoices may simply disappear. To avoid this, you should distribute credit notes against varied invoices. Due to this, only one invoice will not disappear.

Printing Batch Invoices

Sometimes a user may need to print many invoices together at one time. In such cases, it is recommended to utilize the Batch Printing option. To use this option, you just need to create invoices and then click the arrow near the Print option. Next, click on the Print Batch. This will present you with an option to choose the number of invoices to print. This will thus make the whole thing simple and timesaving.

CONCLUSION

Now that we have reached the end of this book, I am sure that by now, you must be well versed with the basics of QuickBooks. QuickBooks is an impeccable software that can help you with all your bookkeeping and accounting needs. This program is really great for people who want to make payments, generate invoices, generate customized reports, create lists for customers, lists of employees, lists of vendors, and export or import data from other applications as well.

As you have now understood the basics of QuickBooks, you can explore it and try to check out various other features of the program. QuickBooks comes with a lot of bells and whistles that make it a great bookkeeping program. It solely depends on you how you use the program.

One of the best things about QuickBooks is that it allows you to sync with the bank account and sync with debit as well as credit cards too. This allows you to stay up-to-date all the time. Whenever a new update comes up, you will stay functional. You can use your up-to-date knowledge to create budgets and keep your financial status healthy. There are many different features that are associated with QuickBooks. These features are good for experts as well as beginners.

The only thing that is left for users to do now is to understand and explore the variety of features and tools of this program. Try to check what features are suitable for you and which are not. You can also customize the program efficiently. You can also customize the lists, statements, etc. You can create lists that are customer-friendly and easy to understand, as well. It does not matter if you are not too familiar with the concepts of techniques and accounting. You can still use QuickBooks efficiently. You just need to check everything and take care of things. This way, you will avoid loss while learning new things. This software can really turn your business around if you know how to use it.